Study Notes on

Romans

Therefore we conclude that a man is justified by faith without the deeds of the law. (Rom. 3:28)

David O'Steen

Study Notes

All rights reserved

No part of this book may be reproduced, or stored in a retrieval system, or transmitted in any form or by any means, electronic, mechanical, photocopying, recording, or otherwise, without express written permission of the publisher.

ISBN: 9798391792574
Printed in the United States of America

All scripture references are taken from the Authorized King James Bible, which is the inspired and preserved word of God in English (Ps. 12:6-7; 2 Tim. 3:16). If this book contains any quotes from modern versions, it is only to demonstrate that they are corrupt (2 Cor. 2:17).

The Study Notes Series

The *skeleton* of information in the Study Notes Series was compiled from my personal Bible study notes. I have worked to *put some meat on the bones* in an effort to make the notes more readable for others. These books are not wordy commentaries, but they are more than just a collection of outlines.

It is my goal to produce material that will promote Bible study, not replace it. The word of God is the final authority.

These were more noble than those in Thessalonica, in that they received the word with all readiness of mind, and searched the scriptures daily, whether those things were so. (Acts 17:11)

Prove all things; hold fast that which is good.
(1 Thess. 5:21)

Study to shew thyself approved unto God, a workman that needeth not to be ashamed, rightly dividing the word of truth. (2 Tim. 2:15)

David O'Steen
Hope Bible Church
Jackson, Georgia

Study Notes

Table of Contents

The Epistles of Paul 5

Introduction to Romans 12

Romans 1 16

Romans 2 40

Romans 3 52

Romans 4 65

Romans 5 77

Romans 6 91

Romans 7 103

Romans 8 114

Romans 9 136

Romans 10 148

Romans 11 157

Romans 12 172

Romans 13 189

Romans 14 198

Romans 15 209

Romans 16 221

The Most Important Question 237

The Epistles of the Apostle Paul

God inspired the apostle Paul to write thirteen epistles, Romans through Philemon, to the Body of Christ in this present dispensation. The church which is the Body of Christ is a spiritual Body wherein there is neither Jew nor Gentile (1 Cor. 12:13; Col. 3:10-11). It was a mystery hid in God (Eph. 3:9) that nobody knew until He revealed it through the apostle Paul (Col. 1:24-27). The Lord also revealed other mysteries to Paul that are related to the Body of Christ (1 Cor. 4:1), such as the mystery of our rapture to heaven (1 Cor. 15:51-52; 1 Thess. 4:15-17).

The Spokesman for the Body of Christ

Just as the law was dispensed through Moses, so the mystery was dispensed through Paul. He is the only writer of scripture who writes about the Body of Christ. No other writer even mentions it! Therefore, it is in his epistles alone that we find the salvation, position, walk, and destiny of the Body of Christ.

We are not exalting the words of Paul above the words of Christ because Paul wrote "wholesome words, even the words of our Lord Jesus Christ" (1 Tim. 6:3). All scripture is given by inspiration of God and is profitable FOR us (2 Tim. 3:16), but it was not all written directly TO us. Therefore, it must be rightly divided to be understood (2 Tim. 2:15).

Just as it was apostasy for Israel to depart from following Moses as their divinely appointed spokesman, so it is apostasy for the

Body of Christ today to not follow the apostle Paul (2 Tim. 1:15; 4:4). In fact, it is apostasy to turn away from the doctrines of grace revealed through Paul to go back under the law of Moses (1 Tim. 4:1-5).

If Satan cannot deceive you into denying the inspiration of the Bible, he will seek to deceive you concerning its proper interpretation. He hates the revelation of the mystery more than any other message because by it God made a fool out of him (1 Cor. 2:6-8). Since it is God's will that all men see the fellowship of the mystery (Eph. 3:9), it is Satan's goal to make sure nobody sees it. He blinds people to the truth by false doctrine and religious tradition.

The apostle Paul referred to the importance of his ministry in every epistle that he wrote. He was not an egomaniac (Eph. 3:8). The Lord placed an emphasis on the distinct apostleship and ministry of Paul because he is the spokesman for the Body of Christ to follow in this present dispensation (1 Cor. 11:1). The failure of the professing church at large to recognize this truth is the reason for all the confusion and division that abounds in Christendom. May God help us to "Hold fast the form of sounds words" (2 Tim. 1:13) of Paul's epistles.

Thirteen Epistles to the Body of Christ

The number thirteen signifies separation (unto bad or good) in the Bible, and it is associated with Paul's ministry (e.g., Acts 13:2, 9). We could say that he was the thirteenth apostle because he was given a ministry that was distinct from the twelve apostles. God inspired Paul to write thirteen epistles to the Body of Christ.

The epistles that Paul wrote are easy to identify because they all contain the same token. False teachers sent out counterfeit letters "as from" Paul (2 Thess. 2:2), so his name appeared in his own handwriting as the first word in every epistle that he wrote as the token of authenticity (2 Thess. 3:17). Many believe that Paul also wrote Hebrews, but not only does it lack his token there are also major doctrinal differences between the epistle to the Hebrews and Paul's epistles (cf. 1 Cor. 12:13; Heb. 3:14).

The Order of Paul's Epistles

The apostle Paul wrote nine epistles to churches in SEVEN (the number of perfection) locations and four epistles to three individuals. While it is not possible to know the exact dates when Paul wrote each of his epistles because that information is not revealed in scripture, we can know the general order in which they were written based on the internal evidence of the Bible.

- During his ministry in the book of Acts (mid to late 50's A.D.), Paul wrote 1&2 Thessalonians, Galatians, 1&2 Corinthians, and Romans.
- During his first imprisonment in Rome (early 60's A.D.), Paul wrote Ephesians, Philippians, Colossians, and Philemon.
- Between his Roman imprisonments (mid 60's A.D.), Paul wrote 1 Timothy and Titus.
- The last epistle that Paul wrote before his execution (mid to late 60's A.D.) was 2 Timothy.

The books of the Bible are not arranged in chronological order, but they are not thrown together by man without order and design. God made sure that Paul's epistles were arranged in a spiritual order that is designed for our edification. Romans was not the first epistle that Paul wrote by inspiration of God, but it is placed first because it is the foundational book of doctrine for this present dispensation.

In the Pastoral Epistles, the apostle Paul gave three faithful sayings that are to be emphasized in the church.

1) Salvation (1 Tim. 1:12-16) – Paul was saved by the revelation of a new gospel.
2) Godliness (1 Tim. 4:8-9) – The mystery of godliness is the Body of Christ (1 Tim. 3:16).
3) Eternal Glory (2 Tim. 2:10-13) – All members of the Body will be glorified, but our reward in how we reign in the heavenly kingdom will be determined by our faithfulness to the truth.

In the last reference that Paul referred to a "faithful saying," he combined all three and provided a definition for what a faithful saying is (Titus 3:4-8). A faithful saying is a statement of truth that is "worthy of all acceptation" (1 Tim. 1:15) and it something we are to "affirm constantly."

The three faithful sayings are related to the three tenses of salvation (justification, sanctification, and glorification) and the three abiding hallmarks (1 Cor. 13:13) of true spirituality (faith, hope, and charity), which are emphasized in Paul's epistles.

The church epistles are arranged according to the order of Paul's faithful sayings. The first four (Romans through Galatians) have to do with the faithful saying concerning salvation. The next three (Ephesians through Colossians) have to do with the faithful saying concerning godliness. The last two (1&2 Thessalonians) have to do with the faithful concerning our hope.

Furthermore, the three groups of Church Epistles are arranged according to the design and purpose of the scripture: doctrine, reproof, correction, and instruction in righteousness (2 Tim. 3:16).

Salvation in Christ – Justification – Faith
- Romans – Doctrine concerning salvation in Christ
- 1 & 2 Corinthians – Reproof for not living by the doctrine of Romans
- Galatians – Correction for doctrinal failure as to Romans

The Body of Christ – Sanctification – Charity
- Ephesians – Doctrine concerning the Body of Christ
- Philippians – Reproof for not living by the doctrine of Ephesians
- Colossians – Correction for doctrinal failure as to Ephesians

The Coming of Christ – Glorification – Hope
- 1 Thessalonians – Doctrine concerning the coming of the Lord
- 2 Thessalonians – Reproof and correction for doctrinal and practical failure as to 1 Thessalonians

Taken together these nine church epistles provide "instruction in righteousness" for this present age.

The first epistle to Timothy and the epistle to Titus concern the proper doctrine and order of the local church. The second epistle to Timothy deals with the apostasy in the last days of this present dispensation.

The epistle to Philemon is fittingly placed last because it illustrates the doctrines of Paul's epistles through a real-life situation.

Paul's Epistles are NOT to be Divided

The Thessalonian epistles were probably the first epistles that Paul wrote by inspiration of God, and yet they are placed last in the order of church epistles because the concern how this present age will end. The mystery of the rapture of the Body of Christ (before the 70th week of Daniel) is only found in Paul's epistles. This proves that Paul knew the mystery of the Body of Christ during the Acts period, otherwise, he could not know and write about our hope.

The same hope in the prison epistle of Ephesians is what Paul taught in his earliest epistle of 1 Thessalonians (cf. 1 Thess. 5:8-10; Eph. 4:4; 6:17 – the helmet of salvation is the knowledge of our hope). This proves that all thirteen of Paul's epistles are written to and about the church which is the Body of Christ and work together as a unit. Understanding this will keep you from becoming a Hyperdispensationalist that wrongly divides Paul's Acts epistles from his prison epistles as though they are written to different groups.

This present dispensation began with Paul's salvation and ministry in the book of Acts, but there are a few differences between the epistles he wrote during the Acts period and afterward due to the transitional nature (i.e., the prophecy program of Israel phasing out while the mystery program of Body of Christ was phasing in) of that period.

For example, Paul went to the Jew first and the sign gifts were in effect to provoke them to jealousy. Paul did not preach the gospel of the kingdom, but God used his ministry to get a remnant out of Israel and into the Body of Christ (see Rom. 11) before He officially set the nation aside in judicial blindness.

The Body of Christ did NOT begin in Acts 28, but the transition period ended.

Introduction to Romans

Romans is the forty-fifth book of the Bible, and it is the first one we come to that was written directly to the Gentiles by the apostle of the Gentiles (Rom. 11:13). Without the book of Acts demonstrating God's transition away from Israel to Paul's ministry among the Gentiles, how strange it would be to go from Christ's earthly ministry to Israel recorded in the Gospel records straight into an epistle to the Romans (Gentiles) from an apostle with a Gentile name! For example, compare Matthew 15:21-28 with Romans 10:12. There are doctrinal differences between the earthly ministry of Christ to Israel and the heavenly ministry of Christ through Paul to the Gentiles (Rom. 15:8, 16).

Paul wrote this epistle around 60 A.D. from Corinth during his three months stay in Greece after his departure from Ephesus (Acts 20:1-3). He wrote it after he had taken up the collection for the poor saints at Jerusalem (Rom. 15:25-26). That Paul sent greetings from saints in Corinth is conclusive that he wrote this epistle from Corinth (Rom. 16:23; cf. 1 Cor. 1:14; 2 Tim 4:20).

Romans was not the first epistle that Paul wrote by inspiration of God, but it is placed first in the order of his epistles because it is the foundational book of doctrine for this present age of grace.

In Romans, we learn that upon salvation we are crucified, buried, and risen with Christ (Rom. 6:3-4). The mystery of the Body of Christ is alluded to but not fully explained (Rom. 12:4-5). The end of Romans (16:25) prepares us for the next great doctrinal book of Ephesians in which we learn that we are seated with Christ in heavenly places (Eph. 2:6).

The key word in Romans is "righteousness" (39x's). This epistle explains how the righteous God can make unrighteous sinners to be righteous saints. This book thoroughly answers the ancient question, **"How should man be just with God?"** (Job 9:2). The words "just," "justified," "justifier," "justification," and "justifieth" appear twenty-two times.

The book of Romans contains great doctrines such as salvation, redemption, justification, imputation, propitiation, sanctification, identification, predestination, adoption, and glorification. All of this and more is offered freely by the grace of God to all sinners everywhere on the basis of the perfect cross-work and resurrection of our Lord Jesus Christ. Believers need to be grounded in these great doctrines. We are saved the moment we trust Christ as our Saviour, but it will take the rest of our lives to learn about all the wonderful things we have in Christ.

The theme of Romans is stated in the first chapter.

16 For I am not ashamed of the gospel of Christ: for it is the power of God unto salvation to every one that believeth; to the Jew first, and also to the Greek.
17 For therein is the righteousness of God revealed from faith to faith: as it is written, The just shall live by faith.

Legalists hate the message of salvation by grace through faith plus nothing. Paul was not ashamed of the gospel Christ revealed to him (Gal. 1:11-12) even though he was slandered for preaching it (Rom. 3:8).

Simple Outlines of Romans

I. Introduction (1:1-17) – The purpose and theme
II. Condemnation (1:18-3:19) – The whole world is guilty
III. Justification (3:20-5:21) – Justification by the faith of Christ
IV. Identification (6-8) – Believers are spiritually identified with Christ
V. Dispensation (9-11) – Israel is temporarily set aside
VI. Application (12-15) – Application of the doctrine
VII. Conclusion (16) – Greetings, warning, and closing doxology

I. Doctrinal (1-8)
II. National (9-11)
III. Practical (12-16)

The book of Romans systematically and logically explains how the righteous God can justify (to declare righteous) unrighteous sinners by faith alone. For example, notice how the following verses build upon one another.

- **<u>Therefore</u> by the deeds of the law there shall no flesh be justified in his sight: for by the law *is* the knowledge of sin.** (Rom. 3:20)

- **<u>Therefore</u> we conclude that a man is justified by faith without the deeds of the law.** (Rom. 3:28)

- **<u>Therefore</u> *it is* of faith, that *it might be* by grace; to the end the promise might be sure to all the seed; not to that only which is of the law, but to that also** which is of the faith of Abraham; who is the father of us all, (Rom. 4:16)

- **<u>Therefore</u> being justified by faith, we have peace with God through our Lord Jesus Christ:** (Rom. 5:1)

- *There is* <u>therefore</u> now no condemnation to them which are in Christ Jesus, who walk not after the flesh, but after the Spirit. (Rom. 8:1)

- **<u>Therefore</u>, brethren, we are debtors, not to the flesh, to live after the flesh.** (Rom. 8:12)

- **I beseech you <u>therefore</u>, brethren, by the mercies of God, that ye present your bodies a living sacrifice, holy, acceptable unto God, *which is* your reasonable service.** (Rom. 12:1)

Romans 1

The apostle Paul had a great desire to visit Rome, and from what he said in the opening passage of this epistle we know that it was not to see the sites, but to preach the gospel of Christ. That was his main purpose in all his travels. God used Paul's ministry to get the gospel to the known world in his generation (Col. 1:6, 23). He could not go everywhere, but he trained many workers and sent them out to places he had not been. Therefore, there were already believers in Rome when he wrote this epistle. In the last chapter he sends greetings to some of his fellowlabourers that were there.

The Introduction

(1) Paul, a servant of Jesus Christ, called to be an apostle, separated unto the gospel of God,
(2) (Which he had promised afore by his prophets in the holy scriptures,)
(3) Concerning his Son Jesus Christ our Lord, which was made of the seed of David according to the flesh;
(4) And declared to be the Son of God with power, according to the spirit of holiness, by the resurrection from the dead:

The opening and closing greetings of Paul's epistles are often overlooked, but there is not a wasted word in the scripture. These passages contain much truth.

Paul's name is the first word in every epistle that he wrote by inspiration of God (2 Thess. 3:17). He said three things about himself in the opening verse.

1) **"a servant of Jesus Christ"** (2 Cor. 4:5) – He referred to himself as a servant of Christ in the first verse of three epistles (Phil. 1:1; Titus 1:1). He was called to be an apostle, but he chose to serve Christ (Acts 9:6).
2) **"called to be an apostle"** (1 Cor. 1:1; 15:9) – Paul typically opened his epistles with a word about his apostleship. He did not magnify himself, but he magnified his office as the apostle to the Gentiles (Rom. 11:13). It is emphasized in the scripture that Paul was called by God to be an apostle because his apostleship was under attack due to his distinctive message and ministry.
3) **"separated unto the gospel of God"** (Rom. 15:16; 2 Cor. 11:7; 1 Thess. 2:2, 8-9) – The word "separated" is used of Paul's ministry three times in scripture (Acts 13:2; Gal. 1:15). God separated him unto a special ministry as the apostle to the Gentiles. He was separate from the twelve Jewish apostles (Gal. 1:11-20).

The most important aspect of separation is what we are separated UNTO. Before his conversion, Paul had rejected Jesus Christ as being the Son of God. Upon his conversion, he was separated unto to preaching the very truth that he had rejected. He now preached the faith that he had once sought to destroy (Gal. 1:23). However, that is not all he preached because he received new revelation from Christ. Romans opens with truth that was "promised afore," but it closes with reference to truth that was "kept secret" until it was revealed through Paul (Rom. 16:25-26).

The Gospel of God

The word "gospel" basically means good news from God (cf. Isa. 61:1; Lk. 4:18). There is only one gospel by which we are saved in this present age of grace (Gal. 1:6-8), but there is more than one message of good news from God in the Bible. The gospel of our salvation is clearly stated in 1 Corinthians 15:1-4.

(1) Moreover, brethren, I declare unto you the gospel which I preached unto you, which also ye have received, and wherein ye stand;
(2) By which also ye are saved, if ye keep in memory what I preached unto you, unless ye have believed in vain.
(3) For I delivered unto you first of all that which I also received, how that Christ died for our sins according to the scriptures;
(4) And that he was buried, and that he rose again the third day according to the scriptures:

Christ sent the twelve apostles to preach the gospel of the kingdom, which was the good news that the kingdom God had promised Israel was at hand (Matt. 4:17, 23; 10:5-7). They were not preaching the good news of the salvation Christ accomplished for all men by His death, burial, and resurrection. By comparing the following passage with the gospel Paul preached, we see that there is more than one gospel in the Bible. The gospel of the kingdom that was preached during the earthly ministry of Christ did not include His death, burial, and resurrection.

(31) Then he took *unto him* the twelve, and said unto them, Behold, we go up to Jerusalem, and all things that

**are written by the prophets concerning the Son of man shall be accomplished.
(32) For he shall be delivered unto the Gentiles, and shall be mocked, and spitefully entreated, and spitted on:
(33) And they shall scourge *him,* and put him to death: and the third day he shall rise again.
(34) And they understood none of these things: and this saying was hid from them, neither knew they the things which were spoken.** (Lk. 18:31-34)

The "gospel of God" is the good news of God about His Son that was promised afore by His prophets in the holy scriptures. It was prophesied that the Messiah would be God in the flesh (e.g., Matt. 1:22-23), that He would suffer, and be raised from the dead (e.g., Isa. 53).

Note the contrasts:
- Humanity = **"made of the seed of David according to the flesh"**
- Deity = **"declared to be the Son of God with power, according to the spirit of holiness, by the resurrection from the dead"**

As a man, Christ was MADE of the seed of David. As the eternal God He existed before His birth (Mic. 5:2). As the Son of God, Christ was DECLARED to be the Son of God, and it was proven by His power, holiness, and resurrection.

It is important to understand that although they are related, there is a distinction between the gospel of God and the gospel of the grace of God (Acts 20:24). The gospel of God was promised in the OT, but Christ revealed a new gospel message to Paul (Rom. 16:25; Gal. 1:11-12). The death and resurrection of Christ was prophesied in the OT, but what all Christ accomplished by it was not fully revealed and preached as good news until Paul's ministry.

The gospel of God is only referred to in epistles that Paul wrote during the transition period recorded in the book of Acts. Throughout the transition period Paul went to the Jew first (Rom. 1:16). He first proved to them that Jesus was the seed of David, the prophesied Christ of Israel. He would show that although Israel rejected her Messiah and crucified Him, God raised Him from the dead, proving that He was indeed Christ, the Son of God (Acts 17:1-3). In this aspect of his ministry, he preached something similar to the other apostles (1 Pet. 4:17, "gospel of God"), but there was still an important distinction.

Peter preached that Jesus was the seed of David and the Son of God that was raised from the dead (Acts 2:22-32). However, Peter preached the cross as BAD NEWS (Israel killed her Messiah), and that Jesus was raised from the dead to sit on the throne of David. Paul also preached that Jesus Christ was the seed of David and raised from the dead (2 Tim. 2:8), but he preached the cross as GOOD NEWS, and that Christ was raised from the dead to be exalted as the Head of one new spiritual Body (Eph. 1:19-23).

The gospel of God is foundational to Paul's gospel. If Jesus Christ was not the Son of God, then His death, burial, and resurrection would not have accomplished our salvation. Therefore, he also preached the gospel of God to the Gentiles (Rom. 15:16).

Although Paul was given a new message and ministry, it is important to understand that it was not isolated from the rest of the scripture. Romans is the foundational book of doctrine for this present age, and it opens with reference to what was promised in the OT. Some think that all we need today is Paul's epistles, but Paul himself would disagree with that (Rom. 15:4; 2 Tim. 3:16).

(5) By whom we have received grace and apostleship, for obedience to the faith among all nations, for his name:

Paul received grace and apostleship from the risen Christ. An apostle was one who saw the Lord and was directly sent out by Him with a message and ministry. Paul received the dispensation of grace as the apostle of the Gentiles (Eph. 3:1-13).

What is "obedience to the faith?" It is the "obedience of faith" (Rom. 16:26). We must put our faith in the faith of God (Rom. 1:17; 3:3). Those who try to work for salvation are not obedient to the faith because it proves they do not believe the gospel revealed to Paul (Rom. 4:5).

In the future tribulation period, the gospel of the kingdom will be preached to "all nations" (Matt. 28:19), "every creature" (Mk. 16:15), and in "all the world" (Matt. 24:14). In present this age, the gospel of the grace of God is to be preached to "all nations" (Rom. 1:5), in "all the world" (Col. 1:6), and to "every creature" (Col. 1:23).

(6) Among whom are ye also the called of Jesus Christ:

(7) To all that be in Rome, beloved of God, called to be saints: Grace to you and peace from God our Father, and the Lord Jesus Christ.

Paul used the word "beloved" thirty times in his epistles. The moment we trust Christ as our Saviour, we are "accepted in the beloved" (Eph. 1:6).

A church is a called-out assembly. All members of the Body of Christ have been called by believing Paul's gospel (2 Thess. 2:14). Being baptized by the Spirit into the Body of Christ (1 Cor. 12:13), we are sanctified (i.e., set apart) in Christ and "called to be saints" (1 Cor. 1:2).

Paul's standard greeting has dispensational significance. In this present age God offers grace and peace to all who will trust Him. The order is always first grace, then peace (Rom. 5:1). After this age ends, there is coming a day when Christ will return to the earth to judge and make war (Rev. 19:11). Have you ever noticed that Paul never sends greetings from the Spirit? The Father and the Son are in heaven, but the Spirit dwells in every believer (Rom. 8:9).

The Explanation

(8) First, I thank my God through Jesus Christ for you all, that your faith is spoken of throughout the whole world.

The apostle Paul gives thanks many times throughout his epistles, and most of the time it is for the saints. He thanked God through Jesus Christ (Eph. 5:20) because all our blessings are in Him (Eph. 1:3).

It was known among the believers throughout the world that there were people in the capital of the Roman Empire that had faith in God's word. A good testimony speaks for itself (1 Thess. 1:8).

The churches in Rome were not established by the apostle Peter, but by fellowlabourers of the apostle Paul (Rom. 16:3-5). If Peter was in Rome, surely Paul would have greeted him along with all the others he mentioned in the last chapter. There is no evidence that Peter ever visited Rome. The Roman Catholic Church, which claims Peter was the first pope, is a false church that began with the Roman emperor Constantine in the third century.

(9) For God is my witness, whom I serve with my spirit in the gospel of his Son, that without ceasing I make mention of you always in my prayers;

Paul suffered much in the work of the ministry, but he kept going because he was serving God from deep within (Rom. 1:15) and not merely going through the motions. Serving God is about more than activity. We know God's truth in our spirit (Eph. 4:23). Those who serve God with their spirit will be faithful to pray (1 Thess. 5:17).

(10) Making request, if by any means now at length I might have a prosperous journey by the will of God to come unto you.

Paul had a strong desire to visit Rome and he prayed for that opportunity. He did make it there by the will of God and the trip was even paid for by the Roman government. He was a prisoner and suffered shipwreck along the way, but he made it safely and so it was a prosperous journey from a spiritual viewpoint. The will of God is rarely easy, but it is always best.

(11) For I long to see you, that I may impart unto you some spiritual gift, to the end ye may be established;
(12) That is, that I may be comforted together with you by the mutual faith both of you and me.

There were evidently some believers in Rome that believed the foundational truth of the gospel of God (Rom. 1:1-4) but needed to be established in the distinctive truths of Paul's message (Rom. 1:15-17; 16:25-27). After imparting the spiritual gift of his message, they would be comforted together in their mutual faith (1 Thess. 5:11).

(13) Now I would not have you ignorant, brethren, that oftentimes I purposed to come unto you, (but was let hitherto,) that I might have some fruit among you also, even as among other Gentiles.

Paul had long purposed to visit Rome. He wanted them to know that he had not made it there yet because of his ministry among the Gentiles (Rom. 15:20-24), and that he desired to have fruit among them also. That Paul would not build on another man's foundation is further proof that Peter did not start the church in Rome.

This is the first of six references in Paul's epistles in which he says that he would not have the brethren to be ignorant of something. Sadly, most of the professing church is ignorant of the very things he told us not to be ignorant about!

1) Rom. 1:13 – Paul's ministry
2) Rom. 11:25 – Israel's blindness and future salvation
3) 1 Cor. 10:1-2 – Baptism = identification, not always water
4) 1 Cor. 12:1 – Spiritual gifts
5) 2 Cor. 1:8 – Trouble in the ministry
6) 1 Thess. 4:13 – The truth about death and our hope

Paul desired to bear fruit for Christ. He mentioned three different kinds of fruit in this epistle.

1) Souls (Rom. 1:13)
2) Righteousness (Rom. 6:22; 7:4)
3) Giving (Rom. 15:28)

(14) I am debtor both to the Greeks, and to the Barbarians; both to the wise, and to the unwise.
(15) So, as much as in me is, I am ready to preach the gospel to you that are at Rome also.
(16) For I am not ashamed of the gospel of Christ: for it is the power of God unto salvation to every one that believeth; to the Jew first, and also to the Greek.

Notice that Paul made three statements that begin with "I am." He did not say, "I was" or "I will." He speaks in the present tense because this was his attitude every day of his ministry. These three statements help us understand his dedication in the gospel ministry.

1) **"I am debtor"** – Paul was fully aware of his responsibility to deliver the message that was committed to him (1 Cor. 9:16-17). Christ died for ALL no matter the color, class, culture, or creed, and therefore all must hear

the gospel. The cultured Greeks considered all Gentiles who did not speak Greek to be Barbarians (1 Cor. 14:11). The Barbarians were uneducated in the Greek culture, but they were not necessarily savages (Acts 28:2). The gospel is simple enough for the unwise to understand it. Those who believe the gospel are responsible to give it to others (2 Cor. 5:17-21). We also have other debts (Rom. 8:12; 13:8; 15:27).

2) **"I am ready"** – Because he was a debtor, Paul was zealous to preach the gospel upon every opportunity (Eph. 6:15), whether to kings or servants. He was instant in season and out of season and gave himself completely to delivering the message committed to his trust (Acts 20:17-27).

3) **"I am not ashamed"** – Paul was always ready to preach the gospel because he was not ashamed of it even though he had been persecuted by the unbelieving Jews for it and the world thought it was foolishness (1 Cor. 1:18). He was not ashamed to preach the gospel of Christ because he knew that it was the power of God unto salvation to all that believe (2 Tim. 1:8-12). Unlike many preachers today, Paul never tampered with the gospel to make it more acceptable to his hearers (1 Thess. 2:1-6).

The gospel of Christ is the good news concerning what Christ accomplished through His death, burial, and resurrection (1 Cor. 15:3-4). On the righteous basis of the finished work of Christ, God has the power to save any sinner who will believe on Him (Rom. 3:19-28).

The power of God is still at work today (1 Cor. 1:18; Heb. 4:12). Taking dead sinners and making them living saints is God's greatest work!

Salvation is deliverance. In salvation we are delivered both FROM and UNTO.

For example, we are delivered:
- From Satan unto God (Acts 26:18)
- From darkness unto light (Col. 1:13)
- From sin unto righteousness (2 Cor. 5:21)
- From death unto life (Eph. 2:1)
- From hell unto heaven (Eph. 2:4-7)
- From bondage unto liberty (Rom. 7:6)
- From the world unto the Body of Christ (Gal. 1:4)

There are three tenses to our complete salvation.

1) Past – The believer HAS been saved – Justification (Rom. 5:1)
2) Present – The believer IS being saved – Sanctification (Rom. 6:11-12)
3) Future – The believer WILL be saved – Glorification (Rom. 8:23)

This great salvation is available to all lost sinners. No works whatsoever are required to receive salvation (Eph. 2:8-9) because Christ did all the work. We must simply trust in His finished work.

To the Jew First

The gospel of Christ was preached to the Jew first during the transition period recorded in the book of Acts. As Paul traveled during that time, he would begin his work by preaching to the Jews in the local synagogue. It was logical to begin by preaching to people who were familiar with the word of God, but the deeper reason was that God had a remnant He was calling out of Israel before He officially set the nation aside in judicial blindness (Rom. 11:1-10). That remnant of Jews believed Paul's gospel and were baptized by the Spirit into the Body of Christ. Of course, Jews can still be saved today, but the gospel is to go out to all men alike, with the Jews no longer being given an advantage.

Israel fell as a nation at the stoning of Stephen (Acts 7:51-60). There was a "diminishing" process as God transitioned away from Israel and revealed the mystery of this present age (Rom. 11:11-15). During this time Paul was careful not to offend the Jews he was trying to reach, which explains certain things he did, like having Timothy circumcised (Acts 16:3; 1 Cor. 9:19-23). The transition period ended when Paul pronounced blindness on Israel when he arrived in Rome (Acts 28:25-29).

(17) For therein is the righteousness of God revealed from faith to faith: as it is written, The just shall live by faith.

In this verse Paul states the theme of this epistle. By inspiration of God, Paul omitted the word "his" from the OT quote (Hab. 2:4) because although we must put our faith in Christ to be saved, we are justified by the faith OF Christ (Rom. 3:22).

The phrase, "from faith to faith" means from God's faith (Rom. 3:3) to our faith. The gospel of Christ reveals a righteousness from God on the principle of faith as opposed to merit, and this righteousness is to be received by faith.

The gospel of Christ reveals how God can be **"just, and the justifier of him which believeth in Jesus"** (Rom. 3:26). How can a righteous God look at guilty sinners and declare them to be righteous? This is an age-old question (Job 9:2; Prov. 17:15). In salvation, God imputes the righteousness of Christ to our account (2 Cor. 5:21). Sadly, many are trying to establish their own righteousness and have not submitted themselves to the righteousness of God (Rom. 10:1-4). Christ also imparts His righteousness through believers as we yield to Him in our daily walk (Rom. 6:18). Paul was falsely accused of preaching grace as license (Rom. 3:8), but he was not ashamed of the gospel of Christ because it is the only thing that gives liberty from sin and makes sinners righteous (Rom. 6:1-4).

The Condemnation of the Gentile World

We have come now to the first main section of this epistle (Rom. 1:18-3:20) which proves conclusively that all are under the guilt and condemnation of sin.

   I. The Condemnation of the Gentiles (Rom. 1:18-32)
   II. The Condemnation of the Jews (Rom. 2:1-3:8)
   III. The Condemnation of the Whole World (Rom. 3:9-20)

Until a person is convinced by the Holy Spirit that they are a lost sinner and absolutely void of true righteousness, they are not ready to trust Christ as Saviour and receive His righteousness.

Therefore, before Paul explains how God saves sinners, he first demonstrates why we need salvation.

It is not possible to really appreciate the grace of God, except against the background of man's sin and God's wrath against sin. Many today water-down the gospel by not dealing with the negative reality of sin and God's wrath against it. Yet, the gospel is about how Christ died for our sins that we might be saved from God's wrath. Therefore, any preacher that will not preach about sin and God's wrath against it has been deceived and is a deceiver (Eph. 5:6). If no one is lost, why preach the gospel?

(18) For the wrath of God is revealed from heaven against all ungodliness and unrighteousness of men, who hold the truth in unrighteousness;

In the gospel, not only is God's salvation revealed, but also His wrath, and both are the revelation of His righteousness. Those who do not receive His righteousness by faith (Rom. 1:17) must face His wrath.

Many take the wrath of God lightly because they are ignorant of what the Bible says about it. Just as we cannot comprehend the infinite love of God that would motivate Him to lay down His life for His enemies, neither can we comprehend the infinite wrath that God will pour out on those who reject His love.

The wrath of God is revealed:
1) **Past** – In time past God revealed His wrath from heaven in a supernatural and visible way (e.g., Gen. 6:11-13; 19:24-25; Deut. 29:23; Ex. 15:3-7).

2) **Present** – In this present age God is not revealing His wrath from heaven in the same manner as He did in the past, but we know about His wrath through His word. We know that lost sinners are "children of wrath" (Eph. 2:3), and if they die in that condition, they will spend eternity in the lake of fire (Rom. 2:5; Rev. 20:14-15). We especially know about the wrath of God against sin by the cross. Christ took the cup of God's wrath on the sin of the world (Ps. 75:8; Matt. 26:39; 27:46).

3) **Future** – The Bible speaks of "the wrath to come" (Matt. 3:7) which refers to God's wrath that will be poured out on the world as never before in the prophesied great tribulation period (Rev. 6:17). The Body of Christ, which was a mystery hid from the prophets, is not appointed to wrath (1 Thess. 5:9) and will be delivered from the wrath to come (1 Thess. 1:10).

God reserves His wrath for His enemies (Nah. 1:2). Who are His enemies? All lost sinners are enemies of God (Rom. 5:10).

In the first verse of a long passage in which all are proven to be under sin (Rom. 1:18), we find a basic definition of sin. It is "all ungodliness and unrighteousness of men." Ungodliness is that which is against the person of God. Unrighteousness is that which is against the principles of God. Ungodliness produces unrighteousness (Rom. 1:21, 29).

How do men "hold the truth in unrighteousness?" This statement will be explained in the following passage (vv.19-23). The modern versions change it to say something like "hinder" or "suppress" the truth as though only those who actively fight against God's truth will face His wrath. All men know some truth through the light of conscience and creation, but many reject it and choose unrighteousness. Those that reject truth become enemies of the truth (v.25).

Verse 18 teaches that a person must reach the condition of accountability, meaning they know good and evil, to be deserving of God's wrath (Deut. 1:39). How could a baby be guilty of holding the truth in unrighteousness?

(19) Because that which may be known of God is manifest in them; for God hath shewed it unto them.
(20) For the invisible things of him from the creation of the world are clearly seen, being understood by the things that are made, even his eternal power and Godhead; so that they are without excuse:
(21) Because that, when they knew God, they glorified him not as God, neither were thankful; but became vain in their imaginations, and their foolish heart was darkened.
(22) Professing themselves to be wise, they became fools,
(23) And changed the glory of the uncorruptible God into an image made like to corruptible man, and to birds, and fourfooted beasts, and creeping things.

The heathen are without excuse because all men have the light of conscience and creation (Jn. 1:9) and thereby have the knowledge:
- That God is real and powerful
- Of good and evil
- That they will be judged by their Creator

The first eleven chapters of the Bible cover the first two thousand years of human history. Consider the light that the world had from God between Adam and the Tower of Babel.

1) Conscience (Rom. 2:14-15)
2) Creation (Ps. 19:1-6)
3) The witness of Adam, who lived for 930 years.
4) The witness of Enoch, who prophesied for 300 years.
5) The witness of Noah, who was a preacher of righteousness and lived 350 years after the flood.

God will send more light to those who receive the light they have. When sinners reject the light of creation and conscience, they plunge themselves into further darkness (Gen. 6:5; Eph. 4:17-19).

In this passage Paul shows the degradation of man. It all began with refusing to glorify God and to be thankful for His goodness (Acts 14:17). The word that describes the story of mankind is not evolution but DEVOLUTION.

Notice the FIVE (the number of death) steps downward:
1) Ingratitude – **"they glorified him not as God, neither were thankful"** – God created us for His glory, and refusal to glorify Him is sin. Ingratitude is a sin that should not be taken lightly. It is the first step to idolatry.
2) Imaginations – **"became vain in their imaginations"** – A mind that is empty of God becomes the breeding ground for vain and wicked thoughts (Gen. 6:5; Eph. 4:17-19).

3) Ignorance – **"their foolish heart was darkened"** – Rejecting light, they go into further darkness (1 Cor. 3:19; Jam. 3:15).
4) Idolatry – **"and changed the glory of the uncorruptible God"** (Acts 17:22-31) – Man was created to worship, and if he does not worship God, he will worship someone or something!
5) Immorality – **"Wherefore God gave them up to uncleanness"** – A wrong view of God will produce a wrong manner of life (Rom. 1:29). Sodomites and lesbians are at the bottom of rebellious degradation. Once a culture accepts that abomination, there is no limit to their perversion.

Notice the degradation of idolatry in verse 23. Instead of worshipping the uncorruptible God, sinners made images of corruptible man, then birds, then fourfooted beasts, and finally creeping things. They changed the truth that there is a God into a lie by worshipping creatures as God.

What was God's response to all of this?

(24) Wherefore God also gave them up to uncleanness through the lusts of their own hearts, to dishonour their own bodies between themselves:
(25) Who changed the truth of God into a lie, and worshipped and served the creature more than the Creator, who is blessed for ever. Amen.
(26) For this cause God gave them up unto vile affections: for even their women did change the natural use into that which is against nature:

(27) And likewise also the men, leaving the natural use of the woman, burned in their lust one toward another; men with men working that which is unseemly, and receiving in themselves that recompence of their error which was meet.
(28) And even as they did not like to retain God in their knowledge, God gave them over to a reprobate mind, to do those things which are not convenient;

This passage provides the historical explanation of why God gave up on the Gentile world four thousand years ago at the Tower of Babel (Gen. 11:1-9). God left the Gentiles to themselves and chose Abraham to begin a new nation (Gen. 12:1-3). In time past, the Gentiles could only come to God through Israel. In the next chapter Paul will show how Israel also rebelled against God.

This passage is not limited to a historical application. It would have seemed to the believers at Rome who first received this letter that Paul was describing their city. The Romans prided themselves on being wise but in reality, they were fools. The city was full of idolatry and immorality.

This passage also has a present application because the same downward cycle is seen in the world today. There are many similarities between the downfall of Rome and America. There is no hope for a culture that has gotten so low and degraded that it rejects the basic truth of what Christ said about marriage.

(4) And he answered and said unto them, Have ye not read, that he which made *them* at the beginning made them male and female,

(5) And said, For this cause shall a man leave father and mother, and shall cleave to his wife: and they twain shall be one flesh? (Matt. 19:4-5)

Because they rejected Him, God gave the Gentile world over to what their own way (Prov. 5:22). This passage says that God gave them up and over to what they wanted THREE times (the number 3 signifies completion). The root problem is stated last (v.28). Wrong thinking produces wrong affections and behavior.

1) Spirit (v.28) – reprobate means rejected (Jer. 6:30)
2) Soul (v.26)
3) Body (v.24)

God never changes in His moral principles. The world is becoming more and more accepting of sodomites and lesbians, but God calls it "vile affections," "against nature," and an "abomination" (Lev. 18:22; 20:13). What is the recompense this error? They are worthy of death (v.32).

There is no such thing as someone being "transgender." Perverted deviants may be crossdressers (Deut. 22:5), but they cannot change their gender. There are only two genders: male and female (Matt. 19:4). We do not help sinners by accepting their sin. They must know they are lost before they can get saved (1 Cor. 6:9-11).

(29) Being filled with all unrighteousness, fornication, wickedness, covetousness, maliciousness; full of envy, murder, debate, deceit, malignity; whisperers,
(30) Backbiters, haters of God, despiteful, proud, boasters, inventors of evil things, disobedient to parents,

(31) Without understanding, covenantbreakers, without natural affection, implacable, unmerciful:
(32) Who knowing the judgment of God, that they which commit such things are worthy of death, not only do the same, but have pleasure in them that do them.

This chapter concludes with an awful list of twenty-three sins that fill the lives of those who reject the truth and are given over to a reprobate mind. In contrast, those who receive the knowledge of God can be filled with the fruits of righteousness which are by Jesus Christ (cf. Phil. 1:9-11).

Many preachers today rarely mention sin, and when they do, they speak of it in general terms. The word of God deals with specific sins. This list includes sins that are both inward and outward, and that are against God and man.

This is not the only passage in Paul's epistles that provides a list of sins (see also 2 Cor. 12:20-21; Gal. 5:19-21; Col. 3:5-9; 1 Tim. 1:9-10; 2 Tim. 3:1-5). This list is like the one in 2 Timothy, but in that passage, Paul describes the condition of the professing church in the last days. Religion does not produce godliness because it is nothing more than an outward form. Where do these sins originate? Christ said it all comes out of the heart of man (Mk. 7:21-23). The evil heart of man cannot be reformed (Jer. 17:9), which is why sinners need to be regenerated by the Spirit (Titus 3:5).

1) Unrighteousness – Not following God's standard of righteousness. All unrighteousness is sin (1 Jn. 5:17).
2) Fornication – Broader than adultery, fornication includes all sexual sin.

Study Notes

3) Wickedness – Delight in doing evil.
4) Covetousness – Not content, the desire for what others have, the love of money.
5) Maliciousness – Wishing harm on others.
6) Envy – More dangerous than wrath and anger (Prov. 27:4).
7) Murder – The act of unlawfully killing a person with premeditated malice.
8) Debate – Strife in arguments (2 Cor. 12:20).
9) Deceit – Purposely misleading others.
10) Malignity – Extreme enmity, an evil heart towards another.
11) Whisperers – Gossip.
12) Backbiters – Running people down behind their back.
13) Haters of God – The desire to be your own god will cause you to hate the true God.
14) Despiteful – Full of spite or maliciousness toward others.
15) Proud – Self-conceit, the first sin (Ezek. 28:17; 1 Tim. 3:6).
16) Boasters – To brag about self.
17) Inventors of evil things – Planning and plotting to fulfill evil desires.
18) Disobedient to parents – A serious sin not to be taken lightly (notice what it is associated with in this list).
19) Without understanding – Foolish (Jer. 5:21).
20) Covenantbreakers – Failure to keep ones promises.
21) Without natural affection – Parents and children mistreating or even killing each other; abortion. Sodomites are without natural affection.
22) Implacable – Unappeasable and irreconcilable.
23) Unmerciful – Unwilling to show mercy to others.

Sinners know in their conscience that they are worthy of death for their sins. Those who are given over to a reprobate mind not only do these things, but they have pleasure in participating in this wickedness with others. The old saying is, "Sinners love company." This passage describes what most Americans watch for entertainment. The brazenness of sinners shows how degraded our country has become. What can we do? Keep preaching the gospel of Christ (Rom. 1:16)!

Romans 2

The natural response of self-righteous religious people to what Paul said about the heathen in the first chapter is to pass judgment on those wicked sinners and proudly boast, "I am better than that" (e.g., Lk. 18:9-14). Paul anticipated that very response.

(1) Therefore thou art inexcusable, O man, whosoever thou art that judgest: for wherein thou judgest another, thou condemnest thyself; for thou that judgest doest the same things.

The Condemnation of the Jews

Paul has proven that the Gentile world is under sin, so now he will prove that the Jews are also under sin (Rom. 3:9). The first part of this chapter (vv.1-16) applies to any self-righteous person ("whosoever thou art"), but when we compare verses 1-3 with verses 17-23, it seems Paul especially had the Jews in mind throughout the entire chapter. The unbelieving Jews thought they would escape the judgment of God simply because they were the seed of Abraham (Mic. 3:11; Matt. 3:7-9).

The Jews were guilty of the same sins as the heathen, and their guilt was even greater because they had more light ("the Jew first," vv.8-9). The fact that they had the knowledge to judge the heathen for their sins brought condemnation on themselves for being guilty of the same things. They hypocritically preached virtue but practiced vice (Matt. 7:1-5).

The same downward cycle among the gentiles can also be seen in history of Israel.

Gentiles (Rom. 1:18-32)	Jews (Rom. 2:1-29)
Without excuse	Inexcusable
God gave them light	God gave them even more light
Truth held in unrighteousness	Truth held in unrighteousness
God gave them up (3x's in Rom. 1:24, 26, 28)	God gave them up (3x's in 2 Chron. 30:7; Ps. 81:12; Acts 7:42)

The Righteous Judgment of God

(2) But we are sure that the judgment of God is according to truth against them which commit such things.
(3) And thinkest thou this, O man, that judgest them which do such things, and doest the same, that thou shalt escape the judgment of God?
(4) Or 41espises thou the riches of his goodness and forbearance and longsuffering; not knowing that the goodness of God leadeth thee to repentance?

This is the only passage in Paul's epistles in which he mentions the need for lost sinners to repent. He also mentioned it several times in the book of Acts (17:30; 20:21; 26:20).

There is much confusion and controversy about the issue of repentance due to the various ways the religious world defines it.

The Catholics turn it into penance (i.e., afflicting yourself to earn forgiveness). The protestants make it to be penitence (i.e., sorrow for sin). Among fundamentalists, many make it sound like a work that sinners must do in order to receive salvation (i.e., sinners must clean up before God will accept them). Some overcorrect in their reaction to all of that and say that sinners do not even need to repent.

If we believe the Bible and allow it to interpret itself, we should have no problem understanding repentance. The problem is that many who are teachers and preachers of the Bible do not really believe it or know how to study it correctly. They use theological books as their authority instead of the Bible. They do not let the Bible define its own words. They do not diligently compare scripture with scripture (1 Cor. 2:13) and rightly divide the word of truth (2 Tim. 2:15).

The first mention of repentance in the Bible teaches us that it is a heartfelt change of mind (Gen. 6:6). That God repented proves that repentance does not mean, "turning from sin" because God has no sin to turn from!

Paul preached that God has commanded all men everywhere to repent (Acts 17:30-31). A sinner must repent in that he changes his mind about sin and decides that he wants to be saved from it. He must repent in that he changes his mind about trusting in idols or working for salvation and decides that he will trust only in the Lord Jesus Christ (1 Thess. 1:9). Faith must accompany repentance (Acts 20:21). We are not saved by repentance, but by the finished work of Christ.

In light of God's goodness, forbearance, and longsuffering toward the Jews, they should have all repented (v.4). Those who did not repent hardened their hearts and will suffer under the most wrath in the day of judgment (v.5). There will be degrees of judgment according to how much light sinners rejected (Matt. 11:20-24).

(5) But after thy hardness and impenitent heart treasurest up unto thyself wrath against the day of wrath and revelation of the righteous judgment of God;
(6) Who will render to every man according to his deeds:
(7) To them who by patient continuance in well doing seek for glory and honour and immortality, eternal life:
(8) But unto them that are contentious, and do not obey the truth, but obey unrighteousness, indignation and wrath,
(9) Tribulation and anguish, upon every soul of man that doeth evil, of the Jew first, and also of the Gentile;
(10) But glory, honour, and peace, to every man that worketh good, to the Jew first, and also to the Gentile:
(11) For there is no respect of persons with God.
(12) For as many as have sinned without law shall also perish without law: and as many as have sinned in the law shall be judged by the law;
(13) (For not the hearers of the law *are* just before God, but the doers of the law shall be justified.
(14) For when the Gentiles, which have not the law, do by nature the things contained in the law, these, having not the law, are a law unto themselves:
(15) Which shew the work of the law written in their hearts, their conscience also bearing witness, and *their*

Study Notes

thoughts the mean while accusing or else excusing one another;)
(16) In the day when God shall judge the secrets of men by Jesus Christ according to my gospel.

This passage reveals some of the principles of God's judgment. It is:
1) According to truth (v.2)
2) Certain (v.3)
3) After longsuffering (v.4)
4) Righteous (v.5)
5) According to deeds (vv.6-10)
6) Without respect of persons (v.11) – no partiality
7) According to the light a person has (vv.12-15)
8) Complete, even to the secrets of men (v.16)
9) By Jesus Christ (v.16)

Many believe that there will be one general judgment that will come at the end of the world. If we rightly divide the word of truth, we will find that there are four main judgments to come. They are different as to who is being judged, when they are judged, where they are judged, why they are judged, how they are judged (i.e., the basis), and what the results of the judgment will be. The common denominator is that the Lord Jesus Christ will be the Judge at all four judgments (Jn. 5:22, 27). God alone has the ability and authority to judge all men.

I. **The Judgment Seat of Christ (Rom. 14:10-12; 2 Cor. 5:9-11)**
   A. Who? The Body of Christ.
   B. When? Upon the resurrection and rapture of the Body of Christ.

- C. Where? In the air (1 Thess. 4:17)
- D. Why? Our service (not sins, all of our sins were judged on the cross).
- E. How? Faithfulness to the mysteries of God (1 Cor. 3:10-15; 4:1-5).
- F. What? Rewards in our reign with Christ in His heavenly kingdom (2 Tim. 4:8, 18)

II. **The Judgment of Israel (Jer. 30:7; Ezek. 20:33-38; Rev. 11:15-19)**
- A. Who? Israel – the first resurrection of prophecy (Rev. 20:1-6).
- B. When? During the 70th week of Daniel and upon the 2nd Coming of Christ.
- C. Where? On the earth.
- D. Why? To purge out the rebels (Ezek. 20:38) and set up the kingdom.
- E. How? Faith and works according to the kingdom program.
- F. What? Rewards in reigning with Christ on earth (Matt. 16:27).

III. **The Judgment of the Nations (Matt. 25:31-46)**
- A. Who? The Gentile nations.
- B. When? The second coming of Christ.
- C. Where? In the valley of Jehoshaphat (Joel 3:2).
- D. Why? To determine entrance into the kingdom.
- E. How? How the Gentiles treated the believing remnant of Israel.
- F. What? Blessing or cursing (cf. Gen. 12:3).

Study Notes

IV.   The Great White Throne Judgment (Rev. 20:11-15)
  A. Who? The lost souls of all ages in "the resurrection of damnation" (Jn. 5:29).
  B. When? After the millennial reign of Christ.
  C. Where? "there was found no place for them" (v.11)
  D. Why? Sin (Rev. 21:8).
  E. How? The books and their works.
  F. What? The lake of fire.

To mix these four different judgments together will lead to confusion and false doctrine.

In this passage (vv.1-16) Paul is talking about the Great White Throne Judgment where all of the lost, of all ages, will be judged on the basis of their deeds (Rev. 20:11-15). If anyone lived in an unbroken pattern of good works and always did it for the right reason, seeking glory, honor, and immortality from God and not in self-righteousness, then God, according to His perfect justice, will give him eternal life. But if not, it will be eternal wrath and anguish that he receives. A man can be justified by the law (v.13) IF he does everything in it all of the time (Gal. 3:10). However, if he offends in point, he is guilty of all (Jam. 2:10). No man, in any dispensation, can live up to God's standard of righteousness and be justified by the works of his flesh (Jn. 6:63; Rom. 3:20).

Those that preach salvation by works misuse verses 6-11 to support their false gospel. The context is about judgment, not salvation. If Paul's point in this passage is to show that a man can obtain eternal life by his own deeds that would contradict the next chapter which plainly teaches that salvation is by faith alone (Rom. 3:20, 28). The point of this passage is to prove that no one can be justified on their own merits. In other words, what is said concerning the condemnation of the world (Rom. 1:18-3:20) prepares the reader for the message of salvation by grace (Rom. 3:21-5:21). As long as a sinner thinks he is righteous, why would he trust In the righteousness of Christ?

In time past, a Jew under the law was required to do the works of the law by faith, but he was not to be self-righteous. Without the sacrifices that God allowed to cover his sins until Christ came to take them away, he would have been damned. When Israel is saved under the new covenant (Rom. 11:25-27), it will be by the grace of God (1 Pet. 1:10, 13). Israel will be justified in the Lord (Isa. 45:25).

That no man can stand before a holy and righteous God in his own merit is a principle that applies in every dispensation (Ps. 130:3; 143:2). At the Great White Throne Judgment, those who lived "without law" (v.12) will be judged on the basis of their conscience (vv.14-15) and will be without excuse (Rom. 1:18-21). Those who lived "in the law" (Jews) will be judged by the law. Those who lived in this present age of grace will be judged by Paul's gospel.

Verse 16 could also mean that God's judgment of lost sinners was part of Paul's gospel in the broader sense of his entire message (Acts 17:30-31). The apostle Paul used the phrase, "my gospel" three times in his epistles (Rom. 2:16; 16:25; 2 Tim. 2:8). It was his gospel because Christ revealed it to him first (Gal. 1:11-12).

Some claim that there is not a burning and eternal hell because Paul did not use the word. The doctrine of hell was established in the Bible before Paul's ministry, and he said that we need

"ALL scripture" (2 Tim. 3:16). Although Paul did not use the word "hell" in his epistles, he described it (vv.8-9, 12; 2 Thess. 1:9).

After laying down the principles of God's judgment, Paul makes a direct appeal to the Jew to prove to him the profound significance of his unrighteousness. The remainder of the chapter brings the argument of the first part to a head.

The Hypocrisy of the Unbelieving Jews

(17) Behold, thou art called a Jew, and restest in the law, and makest thy boast of God,
(18) And knowest *his* will, and approvest the things that are more excellent, being instructed out of the law;
(19) And art confident that thou thyself art a guide of the blind, a light of them which are in darkness,
(20) An instructor of the foolish, a teacher of babes, which hast the form of knowledge and of the truth in the law.
(21) Thou therefore which teachest another, teachest thou not thyself? Thou that preachest a man should not steal, dost thou steal?
(22) Thou that sayest a man should not commit adultery, dost thou commit adultery? Thou that abhorrest idols, dost thou commit sacrilege?
(23) Thou that makest thy boast of the law, through breaking the law dishonourest thou God?
(24) For the name of God is blasphemed among the Gentiles through you, as it is written.

Paul said, "thou art called a Jew" because not all who claimed to be Jews actually were (vv.28-29; 9:6-8). This passage exposes the hypocrisy of the unbelieving and self-righteous Jews, but it also applies to all self-righteous religious people, of which there are still many today.

God had given the Jews great privileges and advantages that they might be a light to the Gentile world (Rom. 9:4-5). Jesus Christ said, "For unto whomsoever much is given, of him shall be much required" (Lk. 12:48). What did the unbelieving Jews do with their privileges?

1) That they rested in the law does not mean they trusted God, but that they thought merely having the law made them safe (Jer. 8:8).
2) They boasted that their God was the true and living God, but they did not know Him (Jn. 8:40-42).
3) They knew God's will as revealed in His law, but they did not obey it (Matt. 23:1-4). The law was more excellent than anything the other nations had, but under grace God gave the Body of Christ something more excellent than the law (Phil. 1:9-11; 3:8).
4) They had the form of knowledge and of the truth in the law, but not the power to keep it from the heart (2 Tim. 3:5).
5) They were self-confident and looked down on the Gentiles who were blind, in darkness, and foolish babes. However, they were in the same condition (Matt. 15:14). In fact, they were under even greater condemnation because they had more light.

The unbelieving Jews thought they were better than the Gentiles even though they were guilty of the same things (v.1): stealing, adultery, and sacrilege (only mention, profaning sacred things, e.g., Mk. 11:17).

God raised up Israel to be a light to the Gentiles, but their hypocrisy and disobedience caused God's name to be blasphemed among them (Isa. 52:5; Ezek. 36:20-23).

Who is a Real Jew?

(25) For circumcision verily profiteth, if thou keep the law: but if thou be a breaker of the law, thy circumcision is made uncircumcision.
(26) Therefore if the uncircumcision keep the righteousness of the law, shall not his uncircumcision be counted for circumcision?
(27) And shall not uncircumcision which is by nature, if it fulfil the law, judge thee, who by the letter and circumcision dost transgress the law?
(28) For he is not a Jew, which is one outwardly; neither *is that* **circumcision, which is outward in the flesh:**
(29) But he *is* **a Jew, which is one inwardly; and circumcision** *is that* **of the heart, in the spirit,** *and* **not in the letter; whose praise** *is* **not of men, but of God.**

Physical circumcision alone did not save the Jews. It was only the sign of God's covenant, and it did not make them righteous in and of itself. Their circumcision did not profit them if they did not believe and obey the word of God.

To illustrate his point Paul gave the hypothetical case ("if") of the uncircumcised fulfilling the righteousness of the law. If that were possible, the uncircumcision would be counted for circumcision of the heart. Of course, the uncircumcised Gentiles were also unrighteous.

What Paul said in these verses about circumcision of the heart is no different than what was written in the law and prophets (Deut. 10:12-16; Jer. 9:25-26). Those who try to keep the letter of the law without believing it in their heart ("in the spirit") are hypocrites.

The word "Jew" is derived from "Judah" which means "praise." The unbelieving Jews sought the praise of men and not of God because they were uncircumcised in the heart.

The final verses of the chapter are typically misused to claim that Gentile believers today are spiritual Jews. Replacement Theology, which is the teaching that church replaced the nation of Israel, is false doctrine (Rom. 11:25-29) that will hinder you from understanding the Bible and who you are in Christ. Israel is NOT the "new creature," the Body of Christ!

To be a spiritual Jew you must start with being a Jew. The saved in this present age are a "new creature" that is neither Jew nor Gentile (2 Cor. 5:16-17; Gal. 3:27-28; Eph. 2:14-16; Col. 3:10-11). There was a distinction in the Acts period between the new creature and the Israel of God (Gal. 6:15-16).

Romans 3

In the last chapter Paul proved that the Jews, who had the law but did not obey it, were guilty before God along with the Gentile world. In the first part of this chapter Paul anticipates and answers three objections of the unbelieving Jews concerning their guilt. He knew exactly how they thought since he used to be one of them.

Answering Objections

(1) What advantage then hath the Jew? Or what profit *is there* **of circumcision?**
(2) Much every way: chiefly, because that unto them were committed the oracles of God.

1) **Objection** (v.1) – What then was the advantage or profit in being a Jew?

   Answer (v.2) – They had many advantages over the Gentiles (see Rom. 9:4-5). Primarily, they were given the law of God (Acts 7:38). God used the Jews to write and preserve the OT scriptures. In fact, it was Jews who wrote the sixty-six books of the Bible.

(3) For what if some did not believe? Shall their unbelief make the faith of God without effect?

(4) God forbid: yea, let God be true, but every man a liar; as it is written, That thou mightest be justified in thy sayings, and mightest overcome when thou art judged.

> 2) **Objection** (v.3) – Did the unbelief of the Jews make the faith (i.e., faithfulness) of God without effect?
>
> **Answer** (v.4) – God forbid! This is the first of ten times Paul says, "God forbid" in this epistle. God is true, but all men are liars. The failure is not with the word of God, but with men who will not believe it (Rom. 9:6). Men may try to judge God, but He is always justified in what He says because He cannot lie (Num. 23:19; Titus 1:2). The reason for the difference between Psalm 51:4 ("when thou judgest") and Rom. 3:4 ("when thou art judged") is that Paul is writing by inspiration of God, and the Lord has the right to make changes when He is quoting His own word to make a point.

(5) But if our unrighteousness commend the righteousness of God, what shall we say? *Is* God unrighteous who taketh vengeance? (I speak as a man)
(6) God forbid: for then how shall God judge the world?
(7) For if the truth of God hath more abounded through my lie unto his glory; why yet am I also judged as a sinner?
(8) And not *rather,* (as we be slanderously reported, and as some affirm that we say,) Let us do evil, that good may come? Whose damnation is just.

3) **Objection** (v.5) – Since the unrighteousness and lies of the Jews demonstrated the righteousness and truth of God, would not God be unrighteous to take vengeance on them for unrighteousness?

Answer (vv.6-8) – God forbid! How could God judge the world for unrighteousness (which the Jews had no problem with) if it were unrighteous for Him to do so? That the truth of God always defeats the lies of men glorifies God, but that does relieve men from the judgment of God. The end does not justify the means in such cases. The slander against Paul (v.8), which is still made against all who preach the gospel of the grace of God, is the philosophy of the carnal mind. As Paul will demonstrate in the sixth chapter, grace is not a "license to sin."

The Final Verdict: The Whole World is Guilty Before God

(9) What then? Are we better than they? No, in no wise: for we have before proved both Jews and Gentiles, that they are all under sin;

This is a definitive passage on the depravity of man. All are under the guilt, power, and condemnation of sin. However, contrary to the false doctrine of Calvinism, lost sinners can still choose to believe the word of God. God has nothing good or positive to say about the human nature. The word "all" is used three times, and word "none" four times for a total of seven which is the number of completion. The Gentiles transgressed God's natural law written in their hearts and the Jews transgressed God's written law.

(10) As it is written, There is none righteous, no, not one:

(11) There is none that understandeth, there is none that seeketh after God.

(12) They are all gone out of the way, they are together become unprofitable; there is none that doeth good, no, not one.

(13) Their throat is an open sepulchre; with their tongues they have used deceit; the poison of asps is under their lips:

(14) Whose mouth is full of cursing and bitterness:

(15) Their feet are swift to shed blood:

(16) Destruction and misery are in their ways:

(17) And the way of peace have they not known:

(18) There is no fear of God before their eyes.

Paul used OT scripture to convict lost sinners of their awful condition (1 Tim. 1:8; Heb. 4:12). In verses 10-12 he referred to Psalm 14:1-3 and Psalm 53:1-3. In verses 13-18 he quoted from Psalm 5:9; 10:7; 36:1; 140:3 and Isaiah 59:7-8. The word of God clearly teaches that man has a sin nature that cannot be reformed (Rom. 5:12; Eph. 2:1-3).

The ROOT problem (vv.10-12) is that the nature of man:
1) Is unrighteous (Ps. 14:1; 53:1)
2) Does not understand (1 Cor. 2:14; Eph. 4:18)
3) Does not seek after God (Ps. 10:4)
4) Is unprofitable (Jn. 6:63; Rom. 7:18)
5) Does not do good (Ecc. 7:20)

The FRUIT that the sin nature (vv.13-18) – The members of the body are instruments of unrighteousness (Prov. 6:16-19; Rom. 6:13):

1) Mouth (vv.13-14) – The words people speak reveal the condition of their heart (Matt. 12:34).
2) Feet (vv.15-16)
3) Mind (v.17)
4) Eyes (v.18)

(19) Now we know that what things soever the law saith, it saith to them who are under the law: that every mouth may be stopped, and all the world may become guilty before God.

How could the whole world be guilty before God when it was only the nation of Israel that was under the law? Jews and Gentiles have the same corrupt human nature. Since the Jews could not keep the law, neither could the Gentiles (Rom. 2:14-15). When the lost stand before God at the last judgment, their guilt will be proven so conclusively that they will not be able to say a word to defend themselves.

(20) Therefore by the deeds of the law there shall no flesh be justified in his sight: for by the law is the knowledge of sin.

The final verdict and conclusion of the first main section of this epistle is that NO flesh can be justified before God by the deeds of the Law because all are under the guilt, power, and condemnation of sin. Why then did God give the law? It was to give the knowledge of how sinful man really is (Rom. 7:12-13).

In the next main section of this epistle, the emphasis moves from condemnation to justification (Rom. 3:21-5:21).

Justification by Faith

Justification is the judicial decree whereby God justly declares a person to be righteous. Justification is not a religious emotion felt by the repentant sinner, nor an experience and degree of sanctity reached by him, but it is the action of God declaring him to be a righteous person. Paul refers to justification twenty-nine times in his epistles and twenty-five of those references are in Romans and Galatians.

How can a righteous God look upon unrighteous sinners and declare us to be justified? That ancient question is the most important question that we need answered before we depart this world (Job 25:4; Ps. 143:2). Sadly, most churches are giving people the wrong answer because they add works to the gospel and thereby pervert it (Gal. 1:6-12). For a person to be justified by the deeds of the law, they would have to keep all of the law all of the time (Rom. 2:13; Gal. 3:10-12). In this passage, the apostle Paul proves that justification is by grace through faith without the works of the law.

(21) But now the righteousness of God without the law is manifested, being witnessed by the law and the prophets;

This is the first of several dispensationally significant "but now" verses in Paul's epistles that sets forth a stark contrast between how God dealt with man in time past and this present age of grace (Rom. 16:25-26; Eph. 2:11-13; Col. 1:24-27).

The righteousness of God is the theme of this epistle. The righteousness of God without the law is a righteousness that is not based on man trying to do the deeds of the law. It is the righteousness which is "by faith of Jesus Christ" (v.22). It is manifested by the gospel committed to Paul (Rom. 1:16-17; Titus 1:2-3). How was it witnessed by the law and prophets? In the next chapter Paul gives two examples from the OT of God imputing righteousness to a man: Abraham and David. But HOW God could do that was not revealed or explained in the OT.

(22) Even the righteousness of God which is by faith of Jesus Christ unto all and upon all them that believe: for there is no difference:
(23) For all have sinned, and come short of the glory of God;

The righteousness of God is available to all sinners, but it is only upon the sinners that believe. All sinners, whether Jews or Gentiles, need this righteousness because all have sinned and come short of the glory of God. Jesus Christ is the glory of God (2 Cor. 4:6). A person might think they are more righteous than others, but our righteousness is dung compared to the righteousness of Christ (Rom. 10:1-4; Phil. 3:4-9). When it comes to sin, that there is no difference between Jews and Gentiles has already been clearly proven in this epistle.

One of the great and distinctive truths that the Lord revealed through the apostle Paul for this present age of grace is what has been accomplished for the Body of Christ by the faith of Christ. Paul referred to the faith of Christ seven times in his thirteen epistles. Yet, this great truth has been removed in the modern versions of the Bible. They all change "the faith OF Christ" to "faith IN Christ." Changing a little two-letter word can make a big difference in Bible doctrine!

We cannot be saved without putting our faith in Christ (e.g., Gal. 3:26), but there is a difference between faith in Christ and the faith of Christ. It should not be surprising that the new versions omit this great truth since they attack the person and work of Christ in a number of passages.

There are different kinds of faith in the Bible (the context determines the meaning):
1) The faith God has revealed to man – A body of doctrine (Rom. 1:5).
2) The faith of God – God's faithfulness and trustworthiness (Rom. 3:3- 4).
3) The faith of a man in God – Believing the word of God (Rom. 1:8; 4:3-5; 10:17).

The faith of Christ covers all three, but the apostle Paul is the only writer who speaks of sinners being instantly and permanently justified by the faith of Christ. The epistle of James and the book of Revelation refer to the faith of Jesus Christ, but both references refer to the doctrine Christ taught in His earthly ministry (Jam. 2:1; Rev. 14:12).

Since Jesus Christ is God, why did He need faith? When Christ was born into this world, He was fully God, and yet He was fully man. As a man, He believed His Father and was perfectly obedient to carry out His will (Titus 1:1-3; Phil. 2:5-8; Heb. 10:5-7). In a book that emphasizes the deity of Christ, we find the Lord continually referring to His dependence and obedience to the Father (e.g., Jn. 5:17-20, 30; 8:28-29). By faith, Christ prayed in the garden, "not my will, but thine, be done" in regard to taking the cup which represented God pouring out His wrath on the sin of the world. He knew that He would be raised from the

Study Notes

dead and that through His death, burial, and resurrection He would accomplish salvation for all who would believe on Him.

Please carefully read the following references in their surrounding context.

1) Rom. 3:21-22 – The righteousness of God by faith of Jesus Christ was witnessed in the OT, not revealed, and explained, BUT NOW is made manifest through the preaching committed to Paul.
2) Gal. 2:16 – God cannot declare a man righteous based on his flesh doing the works of the law (for all have sinned), but He does so by the faith of Jesus Christ which accomplished justification for us by grace.
3) Gal. 2:20 – We are not only justified by the faith of Christ, but we also live by the faith of the Son of God. The Christian life is Christ living His life through us.
4) Gal. 3:22-24 – There was faith in the OT (see Heb. 11), but justification by the faith of Christ was revealed through Paul's ministry.
5) Eph. 3:12 – Because of the faith of Christ, we have the same full and free access to the Father as His beloved Son (Gal. 4:6; Eph. 1:6).
6) Phil. 3:9 – The righteousness that we can try to produce in the flesh is but dung (vv.4-8) compared to the righteousness available to us by the faith of Christ.

The difference between Paul and James on the issue of justification (cf. Rom. 3:28 with Jam. 2:24) is that Paul talks about justification by the faith of Christ, which is perfect and proven, and therefore our justification is instant and permanent; while James talks about justification by the faith of a man, which must be tested and proven by works, and is therefore a process. Paul and James are writing to different groups (cf. Rom. 11:13 with Jam. 1:1) in different dispensations about different gospels.

How many churches believe and teach about what has been accomplished for us by the faith of Christ? Sadly, not many because most do not rightly divide the word of truth and recognize the new revelations that Christ gave the apostle Paul for this present age. Being grounded in this great doctrine produces much assurance of salvation and eternal security (Col. 2:10). Our faith is often weak and wavering, but the faith of Christ is perfect and proven. Rest in what Christ accomplished for you by His faith!

(24) Being justified freely by his grace through the redemption that is in Christ Jesus:

To be justified is to be declared righteous by God. Justification can be offered freely by grace to sinners because of the redemption Christ accomplished through His cross-work (Acts 13:38-39; Titus 3:5-7). To be redeemed is to be bought back from being "under sin" (v.9).

(25) Whom God hath set forth to be a propitiation through faith in his blood, to declare his righteousness for the remission of sins that are past, through the forbearance of God;
(26) To declare, I say, at this time his righteousness: that he might be just, and the justifier of him which believeth in Jesus.

The word "propitiation" is found three times in the Bible (Rom. 3:25; 1 Jn. 2:2; 4:10). Propitiation removes the judicial displeasure of God. It is the appeasing or turning away of the wrath of a righteous God against sin by the acceptance of Christ's death as a satisfactory substitute (Eph. 5:2; Isa. 53:11). Propitiation is applied to us through faith alone. If we have faith in His blood to wash away ALL of our sins, then we will not trust any of our own works for salvation. Without faith in His blood, the wrath of God will come upon the children of disobedience (Eph. 5:6).

The "sins that are past" is not a referring to our personal sins before salvation but to the sins that God covered by His forbearance in past ages since the fall of man. The blood of bulls and goats could not take away sins (Heb. 10:1-4). The remission (i.e., release, forgiveness) of sins is only by the shedding of Christ's pure blood (Matt. 26:28; Heb. 9:22; 10:18). God was righteous in covering those past sins because Christ did come according to His plan and at the appointed time, He took them away.

God is righteous and just to justify us because the blood of Christ took away our sins (2 Cor. 5:21). Who does He justify? All who simply BELIEVE in Jesus. The gospel of Christ reveals the righteousness of God (Rom. 1:16-17). Salvation through Christ is the only way that a just God could justify unrighteous sinners. Since God is just, He would never justify an unrighteous sinner without a righteous basis for doing so.

(27) Where is boasting then? It is excluded. By what law? Of works? Nay: but by the law of faith.

Salvation by faith excludes man from boasting (Eph. 2:8-9). The word "law" is used in this verse in the sense of a principle. If you have not trusted Christ ALONE for salvation, you are not saved.

(28) Therefore we conclude that a man is justified by faith without the deeds of the law.

This is a definitive statement. In this present age of grace salvation is "no more of works" (Rom. 11:6), "not of works" (Eph. 2:8), and "not by works" (Titus 3:5). We are justified by the faith of Christ the moment we believe the gospel of the grace of God. To add any works is to pervert the gospel (Gal. 1:6-12).

(29) Is he the God of the Jews only? Is he not also of the Gentiles? Yes, of the Gentiles also:
(30) Seeing it is one God, which shall justify the circumcision by faith, and uncircumcision through faith.

There is one true and living God who is over both Jews and Gentiles and in this present age He justifies both on the same basis of faith. Some see a distinction in "by faith" and "through faith." However, the words "by" and "through" can be used interchangeably and the point in the context is that believing Jews and Gentiles are justified the same way in this present age.

(31) Do we then make void the law through faith? God forbid: yea, we establish the law.

Does justification by faith make void the law? God forbid. The problem was not the law, but the flesh (Rom. 7:12-13; 8:3).

Justification by faith establishes the law because:
1) The purpose of the law was not justification but condemnation (Gal. 3:24; 1 Tim. 1:8).
2) Christ met the righteous demands of the law and bore its curse for us (Rom. 10:4; Gal. 3:13).

Romans 4

That this chapter begins with, "What shall we say then," (5x's, Rom. 6:1; 7:7; 9:14, 30) indicates that Paul is going to elaborate upon statements he made at the end of the previous chapter about the righteousness of God now being offered to man without the works of the law (Rom. 3:21, 27, 29-30). Paul knew that his Jewish readers would object to such statements, so he used the OT to prove that God imputing righteousness to a sinner by faith is an established scriptural principle. He received new revelations from Christ, but his doctrine did not violate the principles of God revealed in the OT.

Paul used the most esteemed of the Jewish fathers (Matt. 1:1), Abraham (before the Law) and David (under the Law), to illustrate how righteousness without the law was "witnessed by the law and the prophets" (Rom. 3:21). That God could give righteousness to a man by faith was "witnessed" by the OT, but it was not revealed, explained, or declared in the OT.

There are two major false doctrines that are based on a misunderstanding and misinterpretation of Romans 4 and Galatians 3.

1) Salvation in this present age is exactly the same as it was in the OT – The basis (blood of Christ) and condition (faith) are the same, but the message, application, and results are different.

> 2) The church is spiritual Israel – Abraham is our father in the spiritual sense that he is an example of faith. We receive spiritual blessings through his seed, Jesus Christ, but we do not replace his physical seed and inherit their physical blessings. The Body of Christ is a new creature, not spiritual Israel (2 Cor. 5:16-17; Gal. 6:15-16).

Of the nineteen times that Paul referred to Abraham in his epistles, eighteen of the references are found in Romans and Galatians, which are epistles that refute the error of legalism. The unbelieving Jews worked against Paul by telling his converts they were not saved without circumcision and the law.

Since this chapter is about Abraham as an example of faith, let's review the highlights of how God worked in his life.

> 1) After God gave up on the Gentile world (Rom. 1:18-32), He appeared to Abram and made a sevenfold promise (Gen. 12:1-3) by which He would form His own nation.
> 2) Abram began his sojourn by faith at the age of 75 when he and his wife Sarai were childless.
> 3) He was tested by a famine and left the will of God by going to Egypt (Gen. 12:10-20). He lied about his wife to protect himself (again in Gen. 20).
> 4) After returning to Bethel, and separating from Lot, God showed him the land and promised to make his seed as innumerable as the dust of the earth (Gen. 13:14-17). Yet, they still had no child.
> 5) At the age of 85 God appeared to him again and promised that his heir would come from his own bowels and that his seed would be as the stars of heaven for

multitude (Gen. 15:1-6). God confirmed the covenant with him concerning the land (Gen. 15:7-21).

6) Sarai concocted a plan for Abraham to have a son by her handmaid Hagar. At the age of 86 Abram had a son of his own bowels (Ishmael) but it was not the promised seed (Gen. 16:1-5). God did not need Abram's help to fulfill His promise.

7) God did not appear to Abram until 13 (number of rebellion) years later when he was 99. He changed his name to Abraham (father of many nations) and gave him circumcision as a token of the covenant (Gen. 17:1-14). Circumcision is a cutting off of the flesh. It was a token that God would give the seed by His own power and not the work of the flesh. He changed Sarai's name to Sarah (princess) and revealed that the promised seed would come through her though she was barren (Gen. 17:15-22). Abraham laughed at the promise and requested that Ishmael be the seed.

8) The Lord appeared again to Abraham and spoke with him concerning the promised seed and Sarah laughed when she heard it (Gen. 18:9-15).

9) Abraham and Sarah miraculously had Isaac (laughter) when he was 100 years old (Gen. 21:1-5).

10) When Isaac was a young man God tested Abraham by telling him to offer his "only son" up as a burnt offering on Mt. Moriah (Gen. 22). Abraham went up on that mount alone with Isaac to carry out what God instructed him to do. He believed that God would raise him from the dead because he was the promised seed (Heb. 11:17-19). The angel of the Lord stopped him, and God provided a substitute. The passage presents a picture of salvation through substitutionary sacrifice of Christ on the cross.

11) James said that by offering up his son, Abraham was justified by works (Jam. 2:21-24). His faith was tested and proven. Abraham had faith in God many years before. He was declared righteous in Genesis 15, but his faith was made perfect 40 years later in Genesis 22.
12) After Sarah died (Gen. 23) Abraham had 6 more sons by Keturah (Gen. 25) before he died at the age of 175.

Righteousness by Faith: The Illustration of Abraham

a. What shall we say then that Abraham our father, as pertaining to the flesh, hath found?

The Jews boasted in Abraham as their father (Matt. 3:7-9), so Paul used him to demonstrate how God imputes righteousness to a man by faith. God declared Abraham to be righteous four hundred and thirty years before the law was given and while he was yet uncircumcised.

There is some question as to whether the phrase, "pertaining to the flesh" refers to Abraham being the forefather of the Jews (Paul is writing to the Gentiles but makes direct remarks to the Jews – e.g., Rom. 2:17) or if it is referring to what he found out about the flesh. Either sense would fit the context of what is being said in the passage.

Abraham learned that the blessings God promised were not dependent upon his works in the flesh. The works of the flesh cannot please God in any dispensation (Jn. 6:63; Rom. 7:18; 8:8). Without faith it is impossible to please God (Heb. 11:6). God will not justify a sinner by the works of his flesh (Rom. 3:20). Therefore, the flesh cannot glory before God (1 Cor. 1:29).

Justification by faith excludes boasting (Rom. 3:27; Eph. 2:8-9). The Jews gloried in Abraham, but Abraham could not glory before God.

(2) For if Abraham were justified by works, he hath *whereof* to glory; but not before God.

The difference between what Paul and James said about the justification of Abraham is a dispensational one. James, writing to the twelve tribes of Israel concerning the gospel of the kingdom, said that Abraham was justified by works (Jam. 2:21-24). Abraham was declared righteous by God in Genesis 15, but his faith was made perfect by works forty years later when he was willing to offer up his beloved son in Genesis 22. His faith was tested and proven by works. We are justified by the faith of Christ (Rom. 3:22). The apostle Paul, in regard to the gospel of the grace of God, focused on God declaring Abraham righteous by faith. James, in regard to the gospel of the circumcision, focused on how Abraham proved his faith by his works.

(3) For what saith the scripture? Abraham believed God, and it was counted unto him for righteousness.

How was Abraham righteous? He simply believed what God said to him about his seed and God counted his faith as righteousness (Gen. 15:1-6; Gal. 3:8). Since his faith was counted for righteousness, he had no righteousness of his own.

(4) Now to him that worketh is the reward not reckoned of grace, but of debt.

(5) But to him that worketh not, but believeth on him that justifieth the ungodly, his faith is counted for righteousness.

Works cancel out grace (Rom. 11:6). Salvation by grace means that it is a free gift. If God saved sinners on the basis of works, it would mean that He was indebted to sinners. The only thing we deserve is death (Rom. 6:23). Faith is not a work. To believe on Christ for salvation is to trust in His work and not our own. There is no merit in a sinner trusting Christ as His Saviour because he has no righteousness of his own.

By comparing verse 3 ("believed God") and verse 5 ("his faith"), we find that the definition of faith is believing what God said (Rom. 4:17, 21; 10:17).

Righteousness by Faith: The Illustration of David

(6) Even as David also describeth the blessedness of the man, unto whom God imputeth righteousness without works,
(7) Saying, Blessed are they whose iniquities are forgiven, and whose sins are covered.
(8) Blessed is the man to whom the Lord will not impute sin.

Paul referred to imputation eight times in his epistles and six of those references occur in this chapter (Rom. 4:6, 8, 11, 22, 23, 24; 5:13; 2 Cor. 5:19). The word is defined in the context by the synonyms "counted" (v.3, 5) and "reckoned" (v.4, 9). Paul used Abraham to show the *positive* aspect of imputed righteousness, and David to show the *negative* aspect of sin not being imputed.

David, who lived under the law, did not understand how God could do what he wrote about in Psalm 32:1-2. He should have been killed for adultery and murder. The OT prophets did not understand everything they wrote (1 Pet. 1:10-12). He did not understand what was later revealed through Paul concerning propitiation and the remission of sins (Rom. 3:25).

When God justifies the ungodly, He imputes righteousness (positive aspect) to us by faith and does not impute our sins (negative aspect) to us. This blessedness does not come through circumcision (vv.9-12) or the works of the law (vv.13-15). In time past circumcision and law-keeping were required as expressions of faith but neither made a man righteous before God in and of themselves. How can God not impute sins to a sinner, but rather righteousness? The answer was explained in the previous chapter (Rom. 3:20-28) and summarized in one verse: "For he hath made him to be sin for us, who knew no sin; that we might be made the righteousness of God in him." (2 Cor. 5:21)

Righteousness is Not by Circumcision

(9) Cometh this blessedness then upon the circumcision only, or upon the uncircumcision also? For we say that faith was reckoned to Abraham for righteousness.
(10) How was it then reckoned? When he was in circumcision, or in uncircumcision? Not in circumcision, but in uncircumcision.
(11) And he received the sign of circumcision, a seal of the righteousness of the faith which he had yet being uncircumcised: that he might be the father of all them that believe, though they be not circumcised; that righteousness might be imputed unto them also:

(12) And the father of circumcision to them who are not of the circumcision only, but who also walk in the steps of that faith of our father Abraham, which he had being yet uncircumcised.

Abraham was declared righteous fourteen years before God gave him the covenant of circumcision. Therefore, circumcision did not make Abraham righteous but was simply the sign, or token (Gen. 17:11), of his faith in the promise of God. Circumcision is a cutting off of flesh and was given after Abraham depended on his flesh to help God fulfill His promise concerning his seed. The covenant God made with Abraham was all about what God would do with and for Abraham and his seed. His promises will be fulfilled by His power and not by the flesh. How ironic, then, that the Jews would glory in circumcision as though that alone made them righteous. Paul has already proven that circumcision without faith profits nothing (Rom. 2:25-29). The religious world still glories in carnal ordinances (such as water baptism) as though that is what makes them right with God.

Abraham is the father of all who believe, whether Jew or Gentile, in the spiritual sense that he is our example of faith. Jesus Christ told the unbelieving Jews that He knew they were Abraham's seed (physical), but they were not Abraham's children (Jn. 8:37-40).

Righteousness is Not By the Law

(13) For the promise, that he should be the heir of the world, was not to Abraham, or to his seed, through the law, but through the righteousness of faith.

(14) For if they which are of the law be heirs, faith is made void, and the promise made of none effect:
(15) Because the law worketh wrath: for where no law is, there is no transgression.

When God promised to make Abraham the father of many nations (v.17), it was a promise that he would be the heir of the world. God made that promise four hundred and thirty years before the law was given to Israel. Therefore, the promise was given on the basis of faith and not of works. Had it been given on the basis of obeying the law, then faith would be meaningless, and the promise would have been of none effect (Gal. 3:17-18). The law works wrath because all who are under it are guilty of transgressing it (Rom. 5:13-14). The promise is only sure when it is by God's grace and through faith.

Abraham's Example of Faith

(16) Therefore it is of faith, that it might be by grace; to the end the promise might be sure to all the seed; not to that only which is of the law, but to that also which is of the faith of Abraham; who is the father of us all,
(17) (As it is written, I have made thee a father of many nations,) before him whom he believed, even God, who quickeneth the dead, and calleth those things which be not as though they were.
(18) Who against hope believed in hope, that he might become the father of many nations, according to that which was spoken, So shall thy seed be.
(19) And being not weak in faith, he considered not his own body now dead, when he was about an hundred years old, neither yet the deadness of Sara's womb:

Study Notes

(20) He staggered not at the promise of God through unbelief; but was strong in faith, giving glory to God;
(21) And being fully persuaded that, what he had promised, he was able also to perform.
(22) And therefore it was imputed to him for righteousness.

Abraham is mentioned over three hundred times in the Bible. God promised to make his name great and truly he has the greatest name in the world. Jesus is above every name, and one day every knee will bow, and every tongue confess that He is the Lord (Phil. 2:9-11), but many reject Him now. Abraham is highly esteemed by Muslims, Jews, and Christians. His name means, "Father of many" and he has many natural descendants that came through his sons Ishmael, Isaac, and the other sons he had by Keturah after the death of Sarah. But it was through the promised seed Isaac that the nation of Israel came (Rom. 9:7-9). God made a covenant with Abraham concerning that seed being a great nation in the land He promised. as we have already seen, the Israelites that believed God were the children of Abraham.

In this present age Abraham is also the father of all that believe, whether Jew or Gentile, in a spiritual sense (Gal. 3:6-9, 26-29). We receive the blessing of God by faith through Christ who is the seed of Abraham. The Body of Christ is a new creature and not spiritual Israel. We are not a nation that will inherit the land of promise. All who are redeemed by the blood of Christ, both Israel and the Body of Christ, are heirs of the world because we are sons of God. Israel will reign on the earth. The Body of Christ will reign over the earth in heavenly places (Eph. 1:8-11; 2:6-7).

Abraham's example of faith:
1) He believed God concerning things not seen (2 Cor. 5:7).
2) He had hope when all seemed hopeless (Heb. 11:1).
3) He staggered (doubt, waver) not at the promise of God because it seemed impossible.
4) He was fully persuaded that God would do what He promised to do (2 Tim. 1:12).
5) It glorifies God to believe His word (cf. with works in v.2)

How could Paul say that Abraham staggered not at the promise of God? Thanks to the blood of Christ, the sins of the OT saints are not mentioned in the NT (Rom. 3:25). Strong faith is not required for a person to be justified in this present age because we are justified by the faith of Christ. It is not our faith that saves us, but Christ and His finished work.

The Application

(23) Now it was not written for his sake alone, that it was imputed to him;
(24) But for us also, to whom it shall be imputed, if we believe on him that raised up Jesus our Lord from the dead;
(25) Who was delivered for our offences, and was raised again for our justification.

In the final three verses of this chapter Paul draws the spiritual application for us from the example of Abraham's faith. There are things written in the OT for our sake (Rom. 15:4; 1 Cor. 9:9-10; 10:11; 2 Tim. 3:16).

The bodies of Abraham and Sarah were dead as far as procreation was concerned. Yet, Abraham believed God could quicken the dead and give him a son. Just as Abraham believed God concerning things not seen, we must do the same if we too are going to have the righteousness of God imputed to us.

We did not see Jesus Christ die on the cross for our sins and rise again the third day for our justification, but God said that He did. In this present age of grace, the moment we believe the gospel (1 Cor. 15:1-4) we are justified by faith alone (Rom. 5:1).

Romans 5

This chapter concludes the second main section on justification by setting forth some of the blessed results of being justified by faith (vv.1-11) and leads into the third main section concerning our identification with Christ by contrasting the first Adam with the last Adam (vv.12-21).

Results of Justification

(1) Therefore being justified by faith, we have peace with God through our Lord Jesus Christ:
(2) By whom also we have access by faith into this grace wherein we stand, and rejoice in hope of the glory of God.
(3) And not only *so,* **but we glory in tribulations also: knowing that tribulation worketh patience;**
(4) And patience, experience; and experience, hope:
(5) And hope maketh not ashamed; because the love of God is shed abroad in our hearts by the Holy Ghost which is given unto us.
(6) For when we were yet without strength, in due time Christ died for the ungodly.
(7) For scarcely for a righteous man will one die: yet peradventure for a good man some would even dare to die.
(8) But God commendeth his love toward us, in that, while we were yet sinners, Christ died for us.
(9) Much more then, being now justified by his blood, we shall be saved from wrath through him.

Study Notes

(10) For if, when we were enemies, we were reconciled to God by the death of his Son, much more, being reconciled, we shall be saved by his life.

(11) And not only *so*, but we also joy in God through our Lord Jesus Christ, by whom we have now received the atonement.

This passage begins and ends with "we have" (vv.1-2, 11), "through Christ" (v.1, 11), and "by whom" (v.2, 11). We are justified the moment we trust Christ as our Saviour, but it is a life-long process to learn about what Christ did for us and gave us when He saved us. Spiritual growth is not about obtaining what we do not have but learning to walk by faith in all that we do have in Christ. We have a complete standing before God in His grace (Col. 2:10), but we must access it by FAITH.

Being justified by faith, we have:
1) Peace with God
2) Access to God
3) The Hope of the Glory of God
4) The Love of God
5) Joy in God

These great blessings are based on the finished work of Christ, and they are ours by faith. The first three relate to our past, present, and future. Peace with God takes care of the past: He will no longer hold our sins against us. Access to God takes care of our present: we can come to Him at any time for the help we need. The hope of the glory of God takes care of the future: one day we will be glorified together with Him.

This great passage plainly teaches the ETERNAL SECURITY of the believer. All who are justified by the righteousness of Christ will be glorified in His image (Rom. 8:29-30).

Peace with God

All lost sinners are enemies of God that deserve His wrath (v.10; Rom. 8:7-8; Col. 1:21). It is not possible for sinners to make peace with God by our own works. As ungodly sinners without strength, God will not accept anything we offer Him. We are not justified by our works, but by the blood of Christ (v.9). We do not need to make peace with God because Christ made reconciliation (to make peace where there was enmity) for us when He died on the cross for our sins (2 Cor. 5:17-21; Col. 1:20-22). Peace with God is only available "through our Lord Jesus Christ." The corrupt Revised Version teaches that peace with God is not a present possession. It says, "Being therefore justified by faith, let us have peace with God through our Lord Jesus Christ;"

Christ made the atonement for our sins through His blood (v.11). An atonement is the payment that is made to bring two disputing parties together (at-one-ment). The payment is made by the offending party to the aggrieved party. Since in our case, we could not make the necessary payment, the aggrieved party actually became one of us so that He could make the payment for us.

The word "atonement" is used eighty-one times in the OT and just once in the NT. Under the law the blood sacrifice of animals atoned for the sins of the people, but it was not permanent. The atonement that Christ made with His blood is permanent! In the

OT, AN atonement was MADE but in the NT THE atonement is RECEIVED. Israel will receive the atonement as a nation at the second coming of Christ (Acts 3:19-21; Rom. 11:25-27), but we have NOW received it.

The moment we receive Christ by faith we instantly and permanently have peace with God through the reconciliation and atonement that Christ accomplished through the blood of His cross. Our peace with God can never be altered. All believers have peace with God, but not all believers enjoy the peace of God in their daily walk (Phil. 4:6-7).

Access to God

It is by grace that we have a right standing before God (1 Cor 15:1; Eph. 1:6). As a result of this standing, we have full and free access directly to God by faith. This access to God has not always been available to man. Before Adam fell, he walked with God in the garden but after the fall God drove him out. When the law was given to Israel the people "stood afar off" and they were warned not to come near Mt. Sinai "lest they die." In the tabernacle, and later in the temple, there was a thick veil that separated the people from God's presence in the most holy place. Only the high priest could enter once a year on the Day of Atonement. The Gentiles we were even further off from God. There was a middle wall of partition that kept them out, but in Christ we are made nigh to God by His blood (Eph. 2:11-18).

The apostle Paul is the only writer to use the word "access." This access is not through any man, church, or religion. It is only through being a member of the Body of Christ (Eph. 3:12). As children of God, we can go to our Father at any time and for any reason and know that He loves us and welcomes us into His presence. He accepts us as He does Jesus Christ (Rom. 8:14-16).

The Hope of the Glory of God

Our hope is the certain expectation and anticipation of Christ coming for us and being glorified together with Him (Col. 1:27; 3:4). No matter what our circumstances may be, if we walk by faith (2 Cor. 5:7; Heb. 11:1) we can rejoice in hope of the glory of God knowing that the best is yet to come.

Anybody can rejoice in good times. Those who are spiritual glory in tribulations because we KNOW that God does not cause our tribulations, but He can use them for our spiritual growth (2 Cor. 12:7-10; Col. 1:9-13). Getting saved does not remove or even lessen our suffering in this present evil world. In fact, suffering will increase for those who live godly in Christ Jesus (2 Tim. 3:12). If we go through tribulations trusting God, it will produce patience, which provides us with the experience of God's grace and comfort, which gives us hope. We must suffer before we are glorified (Rom. 8:17). The good news is that suffering is temporal, but glory is eternal (2 Cor. 4:16-18).

This is the first mention of the Holy Ghost in Romans. He is GIVEN unto all believers upon salvation (Rom. 8:9). He makes hope real in our hearts (Rom. 8:23-25; Rom. 15:13; 2 Cor. 5:1-8; Eph. 1:12-14).

When Paul said, "we shall be saved" (vv.9-10), he was talking about the rapture (Rom. 13:11). Although we must endure tribulations in this life (Acts 14:22), God has promised that we will not have to endure THE great tribulation that will come upon this world when He pours out His wrath (Rev. 6:17). If Christ would die to reconcile His enemies, how "MUCH MORE" (5x's in this chapter) will He glorify those He has reconciled? By His death we are justified, and by his life will be glorified. We are guaranteed eternal glory with Christ who will save us from the wrath to come (1 Thess. 1:10; 5:9).

The Love of God

That we go through tribulations does not mean that God does not love us or that He is punishing us (Rom. 8:28-39; Phil. 1:27-30). God has already proven His love for us (vv.6-8).

Human love will occasionally go so far as one laying down his life for a friend (Jn. 15:13). In divine love Christ suffered the death of the cross for those who are without strength to serve Him and were ungodly sinners who were His enemies! Therefore, we should trust Him no matter what. We are not ashamed to suffer reproach as we live by faith because the love of God is "shed abroad" (widely, abundantly, not limited) in our hearts by the Holy Ghost (Eph. 3:14-21). The love of Christ constrains us to serve Him (2 Cor. 5:14-15).

Joy in God

The world knows nothing of real and abiding joy for it is the fruit of the Spirit (Rom. 14:17; Gal. 5:22; 1 Thess. 1:6). Because of all that we have through justification by faith (e.g., atonement and hope) we can "joy in God" every day (1 Thess. 5:16; Phil. 4:4). Real joy springs from faith (Rom. 15:13), not feelings or circumstances. It is not based on what is going on around us

(Paul was suffered persecution and was a prisoner), but on Christ who lives within us.

No amount of tribulation and suffering that we face in this present evil world can diminish the unsearchable riches that we have in Christ or prevent us from being glorified in His image.

By One Man

(12) Wherefore, as by one man sin entered into the world, and death by sin; and so death passed upon all men, for that all have sinned:
(13) (For until the law sin was in the world: but sin is not imputed when there is no law.
(14) Nevertheless death reigned from Adam to Moses, even over them that had not sinned after the similitude of Adam's transgression, who is the figure of him that was to come.
(15) But not as the offence, so also is the free gift. For if through the offence of one many be dead, much more the grace of God, and the gift by grace, which is by one man, Jesus Christ, hath abounded unto many.
(16) And not as it was by one that sinned, so is the gift: for the judgment was by one to condemnation, but the free gift is of many offences unto justification.
(17) For if by one man's offence death reigned by one; much more they which receive abundance of grace and of the gift of righteousness shall reign in life by one, Jesus Christ.)
(18) Therefore as by the offence of one judgment came upon all men to condemnation; even so by the

righteousness of one the free gift came upon all men unto justification of life.

(19) For as by one man's disobedience many were made sinners, so by the obedience of one shall many be made righteous.

(20) Moreover the law entered, that the offence might abound. But where sin abounded, grace did much more abound:

(21) That as sin hath reigned unto death, even so might grace reign through righteousness unto eternal life by Jesus Christ our Lord.

In the first main section of Romans, we learned about man's condemnation as a sinner before God. In the second main section we learned about the justification that Christ has provided by grace for condemned sinners. In this passage we will learn that condemnation and justification are both "by one man" (v.12, 15). That is why it begins with the word, "Wherefore" (i.e., for which reason, on this account). It also introduces the next main section concerning our identification with Christ (Rom. 6-8).

This passage opens with the bad news of sin and death in the world by one man, Adam (v.12), but it closes with the good news of righteousness and life available to the world by one man, Jesus Christ (v.21). The word "one" is used twelve times in these verses in reference to one man. A stark contrast is presented between Adam and Jesus Christ. As God looks upon mankind, He sees all people in relation to one of these two men. Everyone is either in Adam or in Christ. All that are in Adam are condemned and will die. All that are in Christ are justified and have eternal life (1 Cor. 15:21-22).

The apostle Paul is the only writer in the NT who takes the issue of salvation all the way back to Adam. Through Adam's fall "SIN" entered into the world. Christ died on the cross to pay for the SINS of all sinners (Rom. 4:25; 5:8), but He also died to solve the root problem of SIN as a nature (Rom. 3:10-18; Eph. 2:1-3). The word "sin" is found forty-five times in Romans, and forty-one of those references are in in the section on identification (Rom. 5:12-8:39). That man has a sin nature made the virgin birth of Christ an absolute necessity!

This passage contains six pairs of contrasting terms:
1) Adam vs. Christ
2) Condemnation vs. Justification
3) Disobedience vs. Obedience
4) Law vs. Grace
5) Sin vs. Righteousness
6) Death vs. Life

There are four reigns mentioned:
1) Death reigned by sin (v.14, 17)
2) Sin reigned by the law (v.21)
3) Grace reigns through righteousness (v.21)
4) The saved reign in life (v.17)

There is an emphasis on abundance:
1) God's gift abounded unto many (v.15)
2) Abundance of grace (v.17)
3) The law made the offence abound (v.20)
4) Sin abounded (v.20)
5) Grace did much more abound (v.20)

The words "much more" are used three times in reference to God's grace (v.15, 17, 20), and five times in the chapter (vv.9-10). In Christ we gain MUCH MORE than what we lost in Adam. We all would have done what Adam did, but none of us could do what Christ did for us. The gift of God is referred to six times, and three times it is called the "free gift" (the corrupt NIV removes "free" all three times).

Notice that verses 13-17 is a parenthetical passage that explains why death reigned before the law was given through Moses. Sin entered the world (v.12) twenty-five hundred years before the law entered (v.20).

Paul's point in verse 13 cannot be that God did not hold sinners accountable for their sins before the law because the scripture reveals that He did (e.g., Gen. 6:5-7; 13:13). The point in the context is that sin is not imputed *as transgression* (first mention in Ex. 34:7) when there is no law (v.14; Rom. 4:15; 1 Jn. 3:4). The law does not make us sinners, it reveals how sinful we are by nature (Rom. 7:12-14). All that are born of the flesh are sinners by nature even if they have no written law. The work the law is written in the hearts of all men (Rom. 2:12-15). The fact that death reigned from Adam to Moses proves this because death comes as a result of sin. A person must reach a condition of accountability before God (knowing good from evil) to be under His wrath (Rom. 1:18). Why, then, do infants die? We live in a fallen world with fallen bodies of flesh.

Two Representative Men

Notice at the end of verse 14 that Adam is said to be "the figure of him that was to come." The tabernacle on earth was but a "figure" of the greater tabernacle in heaven (Heb. 9:1, 6-14, 24). A "figure" is an illustration and representation of something greater (Heb. 11:17-19). Jesus Christ is called the "last Adam" (1 Cor. 15:45-49). In what sense was Adam a figure of Christ? He was the head of the old creation, but Christ is the much greater head of a much greater new creation (2 Cor. 5:17; Eph. 2:10).

Adam and Christ are both representative men. Adam represented all that are born of the flesh, but Christ represents all that are born of the Spirit. There is a stark contrast between the first and last Adam.

1) Creature vs. Creator
2) Natural vs. Spiritual
3) Of the Earth vs. the Lord from Heaven
4) Head of a Natural Race vs. Head of a Spiritual Race

Two Responses to Temptation

The first Adam was disobedient, but the last Adam was perfectly obedient. Adam was created in paradise. He and his wife lived in a perfect environment. They were in a beautiful garden surrounded by food. God had given him a clear commandment (Gen. 2:16-17). Since God created Adam with a free will, he needed to be tested. The serpent tempted the woman. He beguiled her and she in turn tempted the man (Gen. 3:1-6). The root of the temptation was to act independent of God. Adam knowingly and willfully disobeyed the commandment of God (1 Tim. 2:14).

Christ left heaven to be born as a man into this fallen and cursed world that He might redeem what the first Adam ruined. At the beginning of his earthly ministry the Spirit led Christ into the wilderness, and after forty days of fasting in the wilderness He was tempted of the devil (Lk. 4:1-13). The temptation in the wilderness corresponded with the temptation in the garden as to the lust of the flesh, the lust of the eyes, and the pride of life (Heb. 4:15; 1 Jn. 2:16). The root of the temptation was to act independently from the Father's will. The last Adam was perfectly obedient to His Father's will.

Threefold Temptation	Genesis 3	Luke 4
Lust of the flesh (body)	good for food	stones made bread
Lust of the eyes (soul)	pleasant to the eyes	shewed him all the kingdoms
Pride of life (spirit)	desired to make one wise	cast thyself down

The purpose of the temptation (tried, tested – cf. Gen. 22:1; Heb. 11:17) was not to determine whether Christ would sin, but to demonstrate that He was the Son of God and therefore could not sin. Being tempted is not a sin but yielding to it is. There was nothing in Christ to respond to Satan's temptations (Jam. 1:13). Christ was a man, but He was God manifest in the flesh. If there was any chance that He would have sinned, the Father would not have openly declared His approval of Him BEFORE the temptation (Matt. 3:17).

The Bible says that Christ was "without sin" (Heb. 4:15), "did no sin" (1 Pet. 2:22), and "knew no sin" (2 Cor. 5:21). Christ said, "I do always those things that please him" (Jn. 8:29). In the garden of Gethsemane Christ prayed to the Father about the cup He was to drink of which represented God's wrath on the sin of the world (Ps. 75:8). He prayed, "if it be possible, let this cup pass from me: nevertheless not as I will, but as thy wilt" (Matt. 26:39). He was obedient unto death, even the death of the cross (Phil. 2:6-8). Why did He die on the cross? He had no sin. He died for our sins (Rom. 5:6-11).

Two Results

The two responses of the two Adams produced two vastly different results. The disobedience of Adam brought sin, death, and condemnation into the world of mankind. Lucifer, some of the angels, and the woman all sinned before Adam did, but they did not bring sin and death into the world because they were not the representative head of mankind. Through Adam sin and death have reigned in this world. Because he was given dominion over the earth, creation itself was brought under the bondage of corruption through his fall (Rom. 8:20-22).

The aftermath of Adam's disobedience may be summed up with the word RUIN.

The obedience of the last Adam brings righteousness, life, and justification to all that "RECEIVE" His grace (v.17). He offers His righteousness and life as a free gift of His grace. Through the last Adam grace is now reigning through righteousness unto eternal life. God is not presently dealing with the world in His wrath but in grace (2 Cor. 5:17-21).

The aftermath of the last Adam's obedience may be summed up with the word REDEMPTION.

- In Adam: guilt, condemnation, and separation.
- In Christ: no guilt, no condemnation, and no separation.

When God brought Israel under the law, it did not stop or even hinder sin. The problem was not with the law, but with the flesh which naturally rebels against authority. The law was not given to save men, but to condemn them and show us our need of a Saviour. Thank God that His amazing grace abounds beyond our sinfulness! God has been gracious in every age, but in this present age grace is reigning on the basis of what Christ has accomplished for us through His death, burial, and resurrection.

None of us can help being in Adam. We were all born in his image. However, we do not have to stay in Adam. How do we get out of Adam and into Christ? The next chapter reveals the answer.

Romans 6

This chapter begins the next main section of the epistle in which the apostle Paul teaches us about sanctification based on our identification with Christ.

- Romans 6 – Dead to Sin
- Romans 7 – Dead to the Law
- Romans 8 – Dead to the Flesh

W.H. Griffith Thomas wrote concerning these three chapters, "The view of the Cross is thus widened to take in Sanctification as well as Justification, to deal with sinfulness as well as with sins, to apply to what we are as well as what we do; and Sanctification is shown to rest on the same foundation, and to proceed from the same source as Justification, namely, our union with Christ in His death, burial, and resurrection." (St. Paul's Epistle to the Romans, vol. 2, pg. 8)

Romans 6:
    I.   Declaration (vv.1-2) – We are dead to sin (as a nature)
    II. Explanation (vv.3-10) – How it is that we are dead to sin (standing)
    III. Application (vv.11-23)– How this truth is to be lived out (state)

This is a key chapter in the Bible on how to live the Christian life, and it is refreshingly simple (2 Cor. 11:3). Most books and sermons on the victorious Christian life are not based on sound doctrine and they typically make it more difficult than it actually is because they are focused on trying to defeat the flesh by the flesh. There are not twelve steps to victorious Christian living, or even seven steps. There are just three steps as outlined in this chapter.

There are three key words in this chapter: "know" (v.3, 6, 9), "reckon" (v.11), and "yield" (v.13, 16, 19). The teaching of this chapter is summarized in verse 17.

(17) But God be thanked, that ye were the servants of sin, but ye have <u>obeyed</u> from the <u>heart</u> that form of <u>doctrine</u> which was delivered you.

    1) "Doctrine" – Know – Spirit (vv.1-10)
    2) "Heart" – Reckon – Soul (v.11)
    3) "Obeyed" – Yield – Body (vv.12-23)

A Declaration

(1) What shall we say then? Shall we continue in sin, that grace may abound?
(2) God forbid. How shall we, that are dead to sin, live any longer therein?

Paul anticipated and answered the wrong response to what he stated at the end of the previous chapter (Rom. 5:20-21). He knew that the carnal mind would reason, "If the more I sin the more grace God bestows, why not just continue in sin?" That is not the mindset of someone who believes with all his heart that Christ shed His blood and died to take away his sins.

Paul begins this great passage on our identification with Christ by declaring that all believers are dead to sin. We were dead IN sin (Eph. 2:1), but in Christ we are dead TO sin. Yet, he was slanderously reported as preaching grace as a license to sin (Rom. 3:8). Those who preach the gospel of the grace of God should expect the same slander from religious people who vainly think that it is the law that gives people victory over sin. Israel lived under the law for fifteen hundred years and their history is marked by a continual backsliding from God. The law is righteous, but it cannot make us righteous.

Most people seem to either gravitate toward legalism or liberalism. The grace of God teaches us how to live godly in an ungodly world (Titus 2:11-15). Biblical grace does not facilitate worldliness and ungodliness. Salvation by grace is not liberty TO sin but FROM sin. God's standard of living for the Body of Christ under grace is higher, not lower, than it was for Israel under the law. We have a standing and resources that they did not have. Many professing Christians today abuse and misuse the grace and the liberty that we have in Christ. Liberty is not about rights but responsibility (Gal. 5:13).

The professing church today is filled with people who have a form of godliness but deny the power thereof, just as Paul said it would be (2 Tim. 3:1-5). The power of godliness is found in the mystery of godliness (1 Tim. 3:16). The mystery of godliness reveals that sinners are made godly by spiritual union with Christ and not by the religious effort of the flesh.

Real transformation comes from within (Rom. 12:1-2). Do you know the grace of God in truth (Col. 1:3-6; Eph. 4:17-24)? Christian growth is about getting our state lined up with our standing. This is an ongoing process. It is learning to work out by faith what God has worked in us (Phil. 2:12-13).

The Explanation

(3) Know ye not, that so many of us as were baptized into Jesus Christ were baptized into his death?
(4) Therefore we are buried with him by baptism into death: that like as Christ was raised up from the dead by the glory of the Father, even so we also should walk in newness of life.
(5) For if we have been planted together in the likeness of his death, we shall be also in the likeness of his resurrection:
(6) Knowing this, that our old man is crucified with him, that the body of sin might be destroyed, that henceforth we should not serve sin.
(7) For he that is dead is freed from sin.
(8) Now if we be dead with Christ, we believe that we shall also live with him:
(9) Knowing that Christ being raised from the dead dieth no more; death hath no more dominion over him.
(10) For in that he died, he died unto sin once: but in that he liveth, he liveth unto God.

Notice the emphasis on what we must KNOW. At the root of our practical failures in the Christian life is ignorance of the truth of God's word, especially concerning our standing in Christ ("know ye not" is used 12x's in Romans through 2 Corinthians). We do not know about our standing through our feelings and experiences. Sound doctrine is foundational to spiritual growth. We cannot believe and obey truth that we do not know.

We must know that upon salvation we were baptized by the Spirit into Christ, and we are therefore one with Him in His death, burial, and resurrection. Christ already defeated our "old man" (the flesh).

In the Bible, six is the number of man. Romans (6 letters) is the sixth book of the NT (note the word *man* in Romans). This book teaches us how to get out of the man Adam and into the man Jesus Christ (Rom. 5:12-21). The sixth word in the sixth verse of the sixth chapter in Romans is "man." There are six verses in Romans in which the sixth word is man. By the way, the corrupt NIV says "self" in Romans 6:6 and it is the seventh word.

Most professing Christians assume that baptism in the Bible always refers to water baptism. Therefore, they wrongly believe that Paul is talking about water baptism in this passage. If he is, it would mean that water baptism is essential to salvation because this baptism puts us into Christ. That would contradict the first part of this epistle in which we learn that salvation is by grace through faith and without works. The truth is that there is not a single drop of water in this entire chapter.

Water cannot put a person into Christ. Yet, many claim that when Paul referred to the "likeness" of Christ's death and resurrection (v.5) that he was talking about the symbol of water baptism. Paul is talking about a spiritual reality (v.4), not a visible symbol. When Christ was "made in the likeness of men" (Phil. 2:7), was He only a symbol of men? Of course not. Christ was baptized into our humanity that we might be baptized into His Body. To read water baptism into this passage is to destroy its meaning and power in your life. Satan wants us to put confidence in what we can do in our flesh, instead of Christ (2 Cor. 11:3; Col. 2:10; Phil. 3:3).

There are at least seven baptisms in the Bible that differ as to the people being baptized, the element they are baptized with or in, the purpose of the baptism, and the baptizer. There are three baptisms mentioned in one verse (Matt. 3:11): with water (ceremonial purification), the Holy Ghost (power), and fire (punishment). The religious world includes water in how they define baptism, but in the Bible, baptism means identification. In the first baptism God's people walked across the Red Sea on DRY ground (1 Cor. 10:1-2). The children of Israel were identified with the faith of their divinely appointed leader, Moses, when they followed him through the sea.

There is only one baptism that makes us members of one Body, and it is NOT water baptism (Eph. 4:1-6). Upon salvation we are baptized by the Spirit into the Body of Christ. The Body of Christ was a mystery (i.e., secret) revealed to Paul (Eph. 3:1-7). Therefore, the baptism that puts us in the Body was also first revealed to Paul. That Gentiles would be saved was not a mystery. The mystery is that both Jews and Gentiles could be saved by grace through faith alone and thereby baptized by one Spirit into one Body that has a heavenly standing wherein our identity is in our Head the Lord Jesus Christ. Paul emphasized this spiritual baptism throughout his epistles (1 Cor. 12:13; Gal. 3:27-28; Col. 2:12; Eph. 4:5).

We must not confuse the one baptism of the Body of Christ with the prophesied baptism with the Holy Ghost which concerns Israel and the kingdom (Acts 1:1-8; 2:16-18).

WITH the Holy Ghost	BY the Spirit
Prophecy	Mystery
Power	Salvation
Christ the Baptizer	Spirit the Baptizer
Signs	No Signs

We do not have the power to defeat the flesh. Christ defeated it for us once and for all when He died in our place on the cross and rose again. Being crucified with Christ (Gal. 2:20), we are freed from the bondage of sin (v.7, 18, 22).

We do not have to wait for our glorified body to no longer serve sin. We will get a glorified body when Christ comes for us, but in this context, Paul is talking about resurrection power in our mortal body (v.12). Christ lives His life through us as we walk by faith in the newness of His resurrection life (Phil. 3:10). His death and resurrection being inseparable in their purpose and efficacy, union with Him in the one carries with it participation in the other. The Christian life is not just about being dead unto sin, but it is also about being alive unto God.

The Application

(11) Likewise reckon ye also yourselves to be dead indeed unto sin, but alive unto God through Jesus Christ our Lord.

We cannot bring to pass by our faith what God has not done or promised to do. After all, faith is believing God's word, and not just believing. Therefore, reckoning ourselves to be dead to sin and alive unto God does not make it a reality because it already is through the finished work of Christ (vv.1-10). Notice there are both negative and positive aspects to this: dead to sin and alive unto God. They go together on the basis of what Christ accomplished (vv.8-10).

The word "reckon" is a word expressing faith and not feeling. We must reckon (i.e., count it so) in our heart the doctrine we know and yield the members of our body in obedience to the Spirit.

(12) Let not sin therefore reign in your mortal body, that ye should obey it in the lusts thereof.
(13) Neither yield ye your members as instruments of unrighteousness unto sin: but yield yourselves unto God, as those that are alive from the dead, and your members as instruments of righteousness unto God.

We are not to be servants of sin in our mortal body. We do not have to obey the lusts of our flesh (Eph. 4:22; 1 Jn. 2:16). We have a choice (Gal. 5:16). We can LET NOT sin reign in our mortal body, but rather LET the mind of Christ be in us (Phil. 2:5) by LETTING His word dwell in us richly (Col. 3:16). We choose to be servants unto sin or righteousness when we choose to yield (i.e., present, Rom. 12:1) the members of our mortal body to the lusts of the flesh or to the Spirit. Before salvation, we had no choice. Each day we are either yielding the members of our body as instruments of unrighteousness unto sin or as members of righteousness unto God.

(14) For sin shall not have dominion over you: for ye are not under the law, but under grace.

(15) What then? Shall we sin, because we are not under the law, but under grace? God forbid.

Sin has dominion over those who are under the bondage of the law. The law shows us that we are sinners (Rom. 3:20), but it cannot deliver us from sin. Yet, many preachers try to bring people under the law in an effort to fight against sin. The law does not even hinder sin much less stop it (1 Cor. 15:56).

There is nothing wrong with the law when it is used lawfully (1 Tim. 1:8-9). The law is holy, just, and good, but it cannot make sinners holy, just, and good (Rom. 7:12; 8:3). It is like a mirror that shows us we are dirty, but it will not clean us up. The law served its purpose as a schoolmaster, but now God has brought us under something better (Gal. 3:22-28). By grace God gives us the righteousness of Christ and the power to live it out in our daily walk.

It is the apostle Paul alone who declares to the Body of Christ in the word of God that we are not under the law but under grace. What is the fundamental difference between law and grace? It is the difference between demanding performance and offering a gift (cf. Ex. 19:5-6; Eph. 2:8-10).

1) The law said, "Do and be blessed," but grace says, "You are blessed, now go do" (cf. Deut. 28:1-5; Eph. 1:3).
2) The law required righteousness, but grace makes us righteous.
3) The law gave works for man to do, but grace gave words for man to believe.
4) The law cursed sinners, but grace justifies them.

Study Notes

    5) The law was the ministration of death, but grace gives life.
    6) The law is about religion, but grace is about relationship.

God did not put us under grace because He decided to lower or eliminate His standard of righteousness. He put us under grace to enable us by His Spirit to live righteously in Christ. Being under grace raises the standard of living because it means Christ is living His life through us.

To be "under" something is to be in a state of indebtedness, tutelage, and governance. There are many today who talk much about being under grace, but instead of living under grace, they are trying to make grace be under (i.e., subservient) their carnal desires. They try to use grace as an alibi for living worldly and they will accuse any preacher who exhorts believers to live a separated and holy life unto God of being a legalist. The grace of God not only delivers us from the penalty of sin, but also its power in our daily lives (Titus 2:11-15).

(16) Know ye not, that to whom ye yield yourselves servants to obey, his servants ye are to whom ye obey; whether of sin unto death, or of obedience unto righteousness?
(17) But God be thanked, that ye were the servants of sin, but ye have obeyed from the heart that form of doctrine which was delivered you.
(18) Being then made free from sin, ye became the servants of righteousness.
(19) I speak after the manner of men because of the infirmity of your flesh: for as ye have yielded your members servants to uncleanness and to iniquity unto

iniquity; even so now yield your members servants to righteousness unto holiness.
(20) For when ye were the servants of sin, ye were free from righteousness.
(21) What fruit had ye then in those things whereof ye are now ashamed? For the end of those things is death.
(22) But now being made free from sin, and become servants to God, ye have your fruit unto holiness, and the end everlasting life.
(23) For the wages of sin is death; but the gift of God is eternal life through Jesus Christ our Lord.

In this passage Paul uses a common illustration of masters and servants ("I speak after the manner of men") because the infirmity (or, weakness) of our flesh hinders us from understanding deep spiritual truth.

Servants are to submit in obedience to their master. Everyone is a servant to one master (Matt. 6:24). The flesh serves sin. However, since we are dead and risen with Christ, we can now be servants of righteousness. When were lost we were free from righteousness. Now that we are saved, we are free from sin (v.7, 18, 22). However, since we still have the flesh until death or the rapture, it is possible to yield to it instead of the Spirit. If we yield to sin it will lead to more sin (Jam. 1:15) and death (Rom. 8:12-13). If we yield in obedience to righteousness it will lead to holiness and everlasting life (Gal. 6:6-7). Of course, Paul is NOT saying that we earn everlasting life by obedience, because he has already taught us in this epistle that we are saved by grace. We have everlasting life in Christ, but we need to live like it!

When we were lost, we lived a fruitless life doing things that now make us ashamed (cf. Rom. 1:16). But now we can bear fruit to the glory of God (Gal. 5:22-23; Phil. 1:9-11).

The statement in verse 23 is often used in evangelism (and there is nothing wrong with making that secondary application), but the context concerns sanctification. Yielding to sin is death, practically speaking, to the spiritual life we have in Christ. Eternal life, which is the gift of God, can only be lived out through Jesus Christ our Lord.

Romans 7

In the previous chapter we learned how we are dead to sin through our spiritual baptism into Christ which takes place upon salvation. In this chapter we will learn that we are also dead to the law through our spiritual union with Christ.

- Romans 5 – Two Heads: Adam and Christ
- Romans 6 – Two Masters: Sin and Righteousness
- Romans 7 – Two Husbands: The Flesh and Christ

In this chapter the word "law" is used twenty-three times in twenty-five verses. In the previous chapter Paul declared that we are not under the law, but under grace and he explained what it means to serve God under grace. In this chapter he elaborates on how it is that we are not under the law. The law was not made for a righteous man (1 Tim. 1:9; Gal. 5:18). In this chapter Paul demonstrates how that being under the law does not help but rather hinders the Christian life. In Christ we are free to live on a higher and greater plane than the law system.

W.H. Griffith Thomas wrote, "The close connection of this chapter with the preceding one must carefully be noticed, and clearly understood. In 6:21, 22, the apostle has spoken of fruitfulness and service, and these come to the believer by reason of his union with Christ. But something more is necessary in the way of teaching, for this fruitfulness and service can only come and connection with deliverance from law; and, if the apostle did not show this, he would leave the Christian man in bondage, not for salvation, but for sanctification and service, struggling in a hard, legal way to please God, instead of finding his source and spring of joyous service and union with Christ. This instruction about the law is therefore necessary, because of the danger to believers being in bondage to law, and not enjoying the liberty of grace. As we shall see, the conflict of this chapter does not represent the normal experience of the Christian soul, and indeed, only in verses 4 and 6 is there any statement whatever of what Christians ought to be and enjoy in Christ." (St. Paul's Epistle to the Romans, vol. 2, pgs. 29-30)

William Pettingill wrote, "We now come to the 7th chapter, in which it is set forth, that the law being powerless to justify, is equally unable to sanctify. In the first six chapters three wonderful statements concerning the law have been made, namely: (1) "By the deeds of the law there shall no flesh be justified in His sight" (3:20); (2) "The law entered, that the offence might abound" (5:20); (3) "Ye are not under the law" (6:14). These three propositions, as has been pointed out by others, furnish a working analysis of the 7th chapter, as follows: (1) The believer's freedom from law (vs. 1-6); (2) Though the law makes sin to abound, the law nevertheless is not sinful (vs.7-13); (3) The law cannot deliver from the flesh (vs. 14-25)." (Simple Studies in Romans, pg.79)

Dead to the Law: An Illustration

(1) Know ye not, brethren, (for I speak to them that know the law,) how that the law hath dominion over a man as long as he liveth?

(2) For the woman which hath an husband is bound by the law to *her* husband so long as he liveth; but if the husband be dead, she is loosed from the law of *her* husband.
(3) So then if, while *her* husband liveth, she be married to another man, she shall be called an adulteress: but if her husband be dead, she is free from that law; so that she is no adulteress, though she be married to another man.

Some claim that Paul was referring to the Roman law in this passage. In the previous chapters he referred to "the law" thirty-five times in reference to the law of Moses. Why would he all of a sudden be referring to the Roman law here? Paul knew there were Jews in Rome that would read this epistle. They knew what the law said about marriage.

God instituted marriage to be between one man and one woman for life (Gen. 2:24). Notice that Paul did not say the woman HAD a husband, but that she still did when she married another man. By the way, this passage proves polygamy is adultery.

Divorce was permissible under the law because of sin, but it was certainly not permitted for "every cause" (Matt. 19:3-9). There seems to be three legitimate reasons for the marriage bond being dissolved: (1) fornication, (2) desertion, or (3) death (see 1 Cor. 7).

The illustration is simple. Paul used the marriage law to illustrate how believers are dead to the law and joined to Christ. A husband and wife are one until death dissolves their marriage union. Therefore, a married woman is bound by the law to her husband as long as he lives. When he dies, she is free to be married to another.

The Application

(4) Wherefore, my brethren, ye also are become dead to the law by the body of Christ; that ye should be married to another, *even* to him who is raised from the dead, that we should bring forth fruit unto God.
(5) For when we were in the flesh, the motions of sins, which were by the law, did work in our members to bring forth fruit unto death.
(6) But now we are delivered from the law, that being dead wherein we were held; that we should serve in newness of spirit, and not *in* the oldness of the letter.

Death frees a man from the dominion of the law because the penalty of the broken law is death. When that sentence is executed, the law no longer has dominion over that man. Believers are dead to the law by the "body of Christ," which refers to both the physical and spiritual body of Christ. Upon salvation we are baptized by the Spirit into the death, burial, and resurrection of Christ, and His cross-work is the basis for the one new spiritual man that He is building in this age (Gal. 2:19-20). We become dead to the law because our old man is crucified with Christ. We are married to Christ by our spiritual union with Him (1 Cor. 6:17).

Keep in mind that Paul is using marriage as an illustration. He is not teaching that the church in this present age is the bride of prophecy. We are the Body of Christ (mystery), not the bride (prophecy). The godly remnant of Israel will be married to Christ

AFTER the tribulation period (Rev. 19:7-9). We are joined to the Lord the moment of salvation and His righteousness is instantly imputed to our account. We do not have to endure to the end to make ourselves ready for the marriage of the Lamb.

Notice how Paul said that we "were in the flesh" (v.5). The believer is no longer in the flesh (Rom. 8:8-9) because we have been taken out of the old man, the flesh, by a spiritual circumcision (Col. 2:11) and put into the new man, the Body of Christ, by a spiritual baptism (Col. 2:12). When we were in the flesh, we could only bring forth fruit unto death (Rom. 6:21), but now that we are risen with Christ to walk in newness of life, we can bring forth fruit unto God (Rom. 6:22). We now can bear the fruits of righteousness which are by Jesus Christ (Phil 1:9-11). As we learn to walk in the Spirit, we bear the fruit of the Spirit (Gal. 5:22-23) which is Christ being formed in us (Gal. 4:19).

What did Paul mean by "the motions of sins, which were by the law?" Sin is strengthened by being under law (Rom. 5:20; 6:14; 7:13; 1 Cor. 15:56). The problem is not the law, but how fallen flesh responds to it.

We are not delivered from the law because the law is dead, but because our flesh has been crucified with Christ. Serving God in the "oldness of the letter" (under the law) was to serve Him FOR acceptance and blessings. Serving God in the "newness of spirit" (under grace) is to serve Him FROM acceptance and blessings (Eph. 1:3). It is obedience that springs from a new man that sincerely desires to serve God. The letter of the law kills but the spirit gives life (2 Cor. 3:6). Serving God in the newness of the spirit is walking in the newness of life that we have as a result of the Holy Spirit regenerating our spirit (Rom. 6:4; 2 Cor. 3:17-18).

The Function of the Law

(7) What shall we say then? Is the law sin? God forbid. Nay, I had not known sin, but by the law: for I had not known lust, except the law had said, Thou shalt not covet.
(8) But sin, taking occasion by the commandment, wrought in me all manner of concupiscence. For without the law sin was dead.
(9) For I was alive without the law once: but when the commandment came, sin revived, and I died.
(10) And the commandment, which was ordained to life, I found to be unto death.
(11) For sin, taking occasion by the commandment, deceived me, and by it slew me.
(12) Wherefore the law is holy, and the commandment holy, and just, and good.
(13) Was then that which is good made death unto me? God forbid. But sin, that it might appear sin, working death in me by that which is good; that sin by the commandment might become exceeding sinful.

Once again Paul anticipates an argument from his Jewish readers and immediately answers it. He raises the question, "What shall we say?" six times in this epistle (3:5; 4:1; 6:1; 7:7; 9:14, 30). He answers anticipated arguments with, "God forbid" ten times in this epistle.

Paul demonstrates from his own personal experience of being brought up under the law how the problem with being under the law is not the law itself but the law of sin which is in the flesh. The law does not cause sin; it reveals it. The law, as a mirror, reveals sin but it does not clean up the sinner. Being under the law does not prevent or even hinder sin. It strengthens sin in our members (1 Cor. 15:56).

The function of the law is to reveal (1 Tim. 1:8):
1) The fact of sin (v.7) – By the law is the knowledge of sin (Rom. 3:20).
2) The occasion of sin (v. 8) – It gives the opportunity for sin to become exceeding sinful.
3) The power of sin (v.9) – The law reveals how strong sin is in our heart.
4) The deceitfulness of sin (v.11) – Sin promises life and fulfillment but brings death.
5) The effect of sin (vv.10-11) – Sin leads to more sin and to death.
6) The sinfulness of sin (v.12-13) – Legalism breeds rebellion (Rom. 5:20).

When was Paul "alive without the law?" It was before the commandment of the law came into his heart and mind. Once a child reaches a condition (not a specific age) of accountability, knowing good from evil (Deut. 1:39; Rom. 1:18), the sin nature within revives in rebellion against that which is good, and we are dead in trespasses and sins (Eph. 2:1). Those who are without the law have the work of the law written in their hearts (Rom. 2:14-15).

Dr. Peter Ruckman wrote, "When you were born, you were born with a sinful nature, but you were born in innocency. If you had died in that state, you would have gone to heaven. Because you were innocent, God did not impute sin to you; it lay dormant within you waiting for the law to awaken it. That is what Paul meant when he said, "I was alive without the law once: but when the commandment came, sin revived" (v.9). Once sin was awoken by the commandment, God imputed that sin to you because you knew what you were doing, and you freely chose to do it. With sin came the condemnation of the law: death. That is how sin "slew me." (Bible Believers Commentary on Romans, pg. 260)

The Failure of the Flesh Under the Law

(14) For we know that the law is spiritual: but I am carnal, sold under sin.
(15) For that which I do I allow not: for what I would, that do I not; but what I hate, that do I.
(16) If then I do that which I would not, I consent unto the law that it is good.
(17) Now then it is no more I that do it, but sin that dwelleth in me.
(18) For I know that in me (that is, in my flesh,) dwelleth no good thing: for to will is present with me; but how to perform that which is good I find not.
(19) For the good that I would I do not: but the evil which I would not, that I do.
(20) Now if I do that I would not, it is no more I that do it, but sin that dwelleth in me.
(21) I find then a law, that, when I would do good, evil is present with me.
(22) For I delight in the law of God after the inward man:
(23) But I see another law in my members, warring against the law of my mind, and bringing me into captivity to the law of sin which is in my members.

**(24) O wretched man that I am! Who shall deliver me from the body of this death?
(25) I thank God through Jesus Christ our Lord. So then with the mind I myself serve the law of God; but with the flesh the law of sin.**

This is one of the most misunderstood passages in Paul's epistles because it is taken out of context. Many think it describes the normal Christian life. Do you really think that Paul is teaching that it is hopeless for believers to serve God on a consistent basis? In the first six verses of the chapter, we learned that believers are dead to the law and delivered from the law. We can now bring forth fruit unto God by the life of Christ in us. We must keep in mind that in the immediate context (vv.7-13) Paul is describing the results of the flesh being under the law.

Therefore, what he says in this passage (vv.14-25) describes the experience of a man under the law. Paul is speaking as a man under the law to show the inability of the flesh to live victoriously under that system, and to demonstrate why death to the law is part of his message. This prepares the reader for what he has to say about the victorious Christian life in the next chapter.

This passage describes the experience of a man who is trying to be good and holy by his own efforts to keep the law but is beaten back every time by indwelling sin. This is the experience of any man who tries the experiment, whether saved (working for sanctification) or lost (working for justification). The flesh doesn't get saved! It is the flesh is sold under sin (v.14), not the new man (Rom. 3:23-24; 6:7,18,22).

Paul makes three statements about the flesh and backs them up with proof and a conclusion.

I. First Statement (v.14)
  A. Proof (vv.15-16)
  B. Conclusion (v.17)

II. Second Statement (v.18)
  A. Proof (vv.18-19)
  B. Conclusion (v.20)

III. Third Statement (v.21)
  A. Proof (vv.22-23)
  B. Conclusion (vv.24-25)

Paul said that he was not ashamed of the gospel of Christ because it makes sinners righteous, which is something the law could not do (Rom. 1:16-17). It would be a contradiction for him to now say that believers are sold under sin and wretched sinners that cannot do what is right.

Some claim that what Paul said in verse 22 refutes the view that he is speaking as a man under the law. How could this be a description of a believer under grace when Paul has just made the point that we are dead to the law (vv.1-6)? The inward man is referring to the mind. There are many under the bondage of legalism who value the righteousness of the law but fail to fulfill its requirements (Isa. 58:1-2; Rom. 2:17-23).

By saying that this passage does not present the normal Christian life, we are not denying the doctrine of the believer's two natures and the reality of the conflict that exists between the flesh and Spirit (Gal. 5:17). We will experience the conflict between the flesh and the Spirit, but we are no longer servants of sin (Rom. 6:17). If we walk in the Spirit, we will not be in bondage to the lust of the flesh (Gal. 5:13-18).

The flesh is a wretched man and a body of death. Who can deliver us? Thank God for the victory we have through Jesus Christ our Lord!

Romans 8

This is one of the greatest chapters in the Bible, and it concludes the doctrinal section of the epistle concerning salvation in Christ. By inspiration of God the apostle Paul has logically, systematically, and thoroughly explained salvation by faith. He has anticipated and refuted the arguments of the legalists.

- Chapters 1-3 proves all lost sinners, both Jews and Gentiles, are condemned before God.
- Chapters 3-5 explains how condemned sinners can be justified by faith.
- Chapters 6-8 reveals the believer's identification with Christ.

In the last chapter Paul demonstrated the INABILITY of the flesh. In this chapter he declares the ABILITY of the Spirit.

I. Be Spiritually Minded (vv.1-13)
II. We are Sons of God (vv.14-17)
III. The Suffering of this Present Time (vv.18-22)
IV. The Spirit Helps our Infirmities (vv.23-27)
V. We are Secure in Christ (vv.28-39)

The emphasis in this chapter is upon the ministry of the Spirit of God (mentioned 19x's). The victorious Christian life is impossible without the Spirit of God!

As members of the Body of Christ:
1) We walk after the Spirit (v.1, 4).
2) We are made free from the law of sin and death by the law of the Spirit of life in Christ (v.2).
3) We mind the things of the Spirit (v.5).
4) We are in the Spirit (v.9).
5) We have the Spirit dwelling within us (v.9, 11).
6) We have life in the Spirit because of righteousness (v.10).
7) Our mortal body will be quickened by the Spirit (v.11).
8) We mortify the deeds of the body through the Spirit (v.13).
9) We are led by the Spirit (v.14).
10) We have the Spirit of adoption (v.15).
11) The Spirit bears witness with our spirit that we are children of God (v.16).
12) We have the firstfruits of the Spirit (v.23).
13) The Spirit helps our infirmities (v.26).
14) The Spirit makes intercession for us (vv.26-27).

No Condemnation

(1) There is therefore now no condemnation to them which are in Christ Jesus, who walk not after the flesh, but after the Spirit.

Paul uses the word "therefore" twenty-seven times in Romans, which is fitting since he is systematically laying out a logical argument. The adverb "therefore" is used when drawing a conclusion based on what was previously said. There is NO condemnation to believers who walk after the Spirit under grace but based on what Paul demonstrated about the inability of the flesh under the law (Rom. 7:7-25), there is a temporal condemnation on believers who walk after the flesh by putting themselves under the law (7:24; 2 Cor. 3:9).

The last ten words of verse 1 are omitted in most of the modern versions. The translators claim that these words are not in the "best manuscripts." The manuscripts they are referring to, Vaticanus and Sinaiticus, are corrupt. There is a pure stream (Ps. 12:6-7) of manuscripts and a corrupt stream (2 Cor. 2:17). The pure stream of manuscripts does not omit these words. The self-appointed Bible correctors say this is a scribal gloss. They claim that somewhere along the line a scribe that was copying the passage mistakenly took the words from verse 4 and added them to verse 1, and his error has continually been reproduced since then. A marginal note in the Old Scofield Reference Bible says these words are "interpolated" (i.e., inserted or added to the original). Unfortunately, that is not the only note in the Scofield Bible that casts doubt on the word of God (e.g., see the notes on Mk. 16:9-20 and 1 Jn. 5:7).

This is just a classic example of men changing God's word when they do not understand it. Because they do not understand the verse in its context, they think it is implying that a believer can lose salvation. Therefore, they change it to match their limited understanding. We must change our beliefs to match the word of God, and never change the word of God to match our beliefs. We must believe what the Bible says even if we do not understand it. God will give us further light as we study His word with a BELIEVING heart.

The King James Bible is perfect because it is the inspired word of God in the English language. To alter one word is to throw things out of sorts and cause a real problem. God's word is exact and precise. In the immediate context, we have an example of the precision of God's word (v.3).

"God sending his own Son in the likeness of sinful flesh"

It would not have been doctrinally sound to say:
1) *"in sinful flesh"* because He was without sin
2) *"in the likeness of flesh"* because He came in actual flesh
3) *"in the flesh"* because He has an immortal flesh and bone body after the resurrection that was not in the likeness of sinful flesh

In the light of the doctrine set forth in the first eight chapters, we know that verse 1 cannot mean that it is possible for a member of the Body of Christ to lose salvation. This very chapter teaches the eternal security of the believer (Rom. 8:28-39). So, what is the point?

There is no eternal condemnation to those who are in Christ. However, a believer can bring temporal condemnation (e.g., Rom. 14:22-23; 1 Cor. 11:27-34; 1 Tim. 5:12) on himself in this life if he gives place to the flesh and puts himself back under the law. This has to do with our temporal state (changeable condition) and not our eternal standing (unchangeable position in Christ). Those who walk after the Spirit do not put themselves under the law (Gal. 5:18).

It Is also possible that the clause, "who walk not after the flesh, but after the Spirit" is a descriptive clause and not a conditional one. The Spirit of God has led ALL believers put their trust in Christ (v.14), but we do not always walk in the Spirit as we should.

A Greater Law

(2) For the law of the Spirit of life in Christ Jesus hath made me free from the law of sin and death.
(3) For what the law could not do, in that it was weak through the flesh, God sending his own Son in the likeness of sinful flesh, and for sin, condemned sin in the flesh:
(4) That the righteousness of the law might be fulfilled in us, who walk not after the flesh, but after the Spirit.

There are three different laws mentioned in these verses. In the Bible the word "law" does not always refer to the law of Moses. A law is a fixed rule or principle; the context determines which law is referred to. That we are "not under the law" (Rom. 6:14) does not mean we are to live lawlessly. We are "not without law to God, but under the law to Christ" (1 Cor. 9:21). We are to operate under a greater law that superseded the law of Moses: the law of the Spirit of life in Christ Jesus.

There are seven different laws mentioned in Romans 1-8:
1) The law (2:12) – The law God revealed through Moses.
2) The law of faith (3:27) – The principle of justification by faith.
3) The law of ever present evil when trying to do good (7:21).
4) The law of the mind (7:23) – Our mindset.
5) The law of sin in our members (7:23) – Sin dwells in our body.
6) The law of sin and death (8:2) – Sin is the nature of the flesh, and it brings death.

7) The law of the Spirit of life in Christ Jesus (8:2) – The Spirit gives life through the righteousness of Christ. This greater law delivers those in Christ from the law of sin and death.

Since Christ was condemned in our place (v.3) and we have His righteousness (v.4), it is impossible for a member of His Body to be eternally condemned (vv.33-34).

In sending His own Son in the likeness of sinful flesh to condemn sin on the cross, God accomplished for us what the law could not do. The problem with the law is the inability of the flesh to keep it (vv.7-8). Christ took away our sin that He might give us His righteousness. The righteousness of the law is fulfilled in those who are led of the Spirit to put their trust in Christ.

Carnally Minded vs. Spiritually Minded

(5) For they that are after the flesh do mind the things of the flesh; but they that are after the Spirit the things of the Spirit.
(6) For to be carnally minded is death; but to be spiritually minded is life and peace.
(7) Because the carnal mind is enmity against God: for it is not subject to the law of God, neither indeed can be.

Those that walk after the flesh set their affection upon and seek to live according to the things of the flesh. In this context, the "things of the flesh" are the religious ordinances of the law that can be performed by the flesh (Phil. 3:7-9, 18-19; Heb. 9:1, 10).

Those that walk are after the Spirit set their affection upon and seek to live according to the things of the Spirit (Col. 3:1-4), which refer to the spiritual blessings (Eph. 1:3) we have as members of the Body of Christ (1 Cor. 2:6-16).

The carnal mind is death, practically speaking (Eph. 5:14), because it relies upon the flesh which is at enmity with God and cannot be righteous (as was demonstrated in Rom. 7:14-24). The spiritual mind is life and peace because it rests on the righteousness of Christ (Rom. 5:1). The issue is the mind because that is the battlefield in spiritual warfare (2 Cor. 10:5; 11:3). What we believe determines how we live.

In the Flesh vs. In the Spirit

(8) So then they that are in the flesh cannot please God.
(9) But ye are not in the flesh, but in the Spirit, if so be that the Spirit of God dwell in you. Now if any man have not the Spirit of Christ, he is none of his.
(10) And if Christ be in you, the body is dead because of sin; but the Spirit is life because of righteousness.
(11) But if the Spirit of him that raised up Jesus from the dead dwell in you, he that raised up Christ from the dead shall also quicken your mortal bodies by his Spirit that dwelleth in you.

All men are either in the flesh (Adam) or in the Spirit (Christ). Those that are in the flesh cannot please God because the flesh is totally corrupt (Rom. 7:18). Therefore, it is impossible for a lost sinner to earn justification or sanctification by the works of the flesh. We can only please God by faith (Heb. 11:6).

Paul has already explained how it is that we are not in the flesh but in the Spirit (Rom. 6:3-4). The moment we trust Jesus Christ as our Saviour we are taken out of the flesh by a spiritual circumcision (Col. 2:11) and put into Christ by a spiritual baptism (Col. 2:12). We are sealed with the Spirit until the redemption of our body (v.23; Eph. 4:30). Therefore, as to our spiritual standing before God, we are no longer in the flesh but in the Spirit. All believers are in the Spirit, but not all walk in the Spirit (Gal. 5:25).

As to our standing ALL believers have the Spirit of God dwelling in them as a permanent resident (1 Cor. 3:16; 6:19; Eph. 4:30). The Spirit dwelling in us is defined in the context as having the Spirit. That the Spirit of God is also the Spirit of Christ proves that Christ is God. Christ lives in us by His Spirit (Col. 1:27). That sin dwells in our flesh is no excuse to serve sin since the Spirit also dwells in us. As to our state, Christ dwells in us by faith (Gal. 4:19; Eph. 3:17) in proportion to His word dwelling in us (Col. 3:16).

We live in a body of death (Rom. 7:24; 2 Cor. 4:16) but we have life in the Spirit because of the righteousness of Christ. That the Spirit dwells in us is the guarantee that He will one day also quicken our mortal body (v.23; Eph. 1:13-14). Until then He gives the resurrection power to walk in newness of life (6:3-4; Eph. 1:19-20).

Debtors

(12) Therefore, brethren, we are debtors, not to the flesh, to live after the flesh.

(13) For if ye live after the flesh, ye shall die: but if ye through the Spirit do mortify the deeds of the body, ye shall live.

We do not owe the flesh anything because it is dead, and we are no longer in it. Being "UNDER grace" we are debtors to the Spirit because we are in Him, and we have life in Him. Those who are carnally minded live after the flesh. What does that produce? It results in practical death to our spiritual walk and fruitfulness. Those who through the Spirit put to death the deeds of the body (Col. 3:5) live the Christian life. How do we mortify the deeds of the body through the Spirit? It is NOT by religious discipline (Col. 2:20-23), but by walking in the Spirit (Gal. 5:16).

Sons of God

(14) For as many as are led by the Spirit of God, they are the sons of God.
(15) For ye have not received the spirit of bondage again to fear; but ye have received the Spirit of adoption, whereby we cry, Abba, Father.
(16) The Spirit itself beareth witness with our spirit, that we are the children of God:
(17) And if children, then heirs; heirs of God, and joint-heirs with Christ; if so be that we suffer with him, that we may be also glorified together.

All believers are led by the Spirit of God, but not all believers walk after the Spirit. The sons of God are those whom the Spirit of God has led by the word of God to put their trust in the finished work of Christ (Gal. 3:26; 5:18). We did not become sons of God by the works of the flesh (Titus 3:5). The Spirit does not lead people to the law for justification or sanctification (Gal. 3:1-3).

The carnally minded walk after the spirit of bondage, but the spiritually minded walk after the Spirit of adoption. What is the "spirit of bondage?" Later in this passage Paul mentions the "bondage of corruption" (v.21) but that is not a spiritual bondage. The "spirit of bondage" refers to the bondage of being under the law (Gal. 5:1) as described in the previous chapter. It is the spirit that religious people have before they are saved ("again"). The law produces fear and not confidence because it condemns and kills us. God did not save us to put us back under the bondage of the law. We are delivered from the law (Rom. 7:6).

Since the law brings bondage, how could James call it a "law of liberty" (Jam. 1:25; 2:10-12)? It will not be a yoke of bondage for those who are filled with the Holy Ghost (Ezek. 36:22-28). Israel will keep the ordinances of the law in the kingdom. We are not under the ordinances of the law (Col. 2:13-17) and the Holy Ghost will not cause us to keep the law. We are as filled with the Spirit as we are yielded to Him and filled with the word of God (Eph. 5:18-21; Col. 3:16).

As sons of God, we have received the Spirit of adoption. It is the Spirit of God dwelling in us that proves we have been adopted (v.9). The word "adoption" is found five times in the Bible, and all five references are found in Paul's epistles (Rom. 8:15, 23; 9:4; Gal. 4:5; Eph. 1:5).

In the Bible, adoption is not used in the sense of making someone a child who was not born into the family. We were born into the family of God upon salvation. Adoption is the full placement as a son. It has to do with position and the rights, privileges, and responsibilities that come with that position (Gal. 4:1-11). Being complete in Christ we have this position now, but we have yet to fully enter the experience of all it means to be a son of God.

Paul speaks of adoption in relation to the Body of Christ in three passages and applies it in three tenses.

1) As to the past, we were predestinated unto adoption (Eph. 1:3-6).
2) As to the present, we now have the Spirit of adoption (Rom. 8:15; Gal. 4:5-6).
3) As to the future, we are waiting for adoption (Rom. 8:23).

The Aramaic word "Abba" is untranslated because it a special term for *Father* that is only used three times in the NT in the context of prayer. This is what Jesus called the Father when He was praying in Gethsemane (Mk. 14:36). We cry "Abba, Father" because we are accepted in the beloved (Mk. 1:11; Eph. 1:6). What an amazing thing that Gentiles (Eph. 2:12, 18; 3:12) can have a personal relationship with the Father!

Notice that verse 16 says that the Spirit bears witness WITH our spirit and not TO our spirit. As we cry "Abba, Father," the Spirit bears witness with our spirit to the Father we are His children. He prays with us and for us (Rom. 8:26).

Why does the KJB refer to the Spirit of God as "itself" since He is a person? It is a literal and correct translation. In the context the WORK of the Spirit is set in contrast with non-personal things

Being children of God makes us heirs of God (eternal life, Titus 3:7) and joint-heirs with Christ. The unrighteous have no inheritance (1 Cor. 6:9-11; Eph. 5:5-11). All members of the Body of Christ are joint-heirs with Christ. Being a joint-heir does not mean we split the inheritance with Christ but that we inherit all that He does. What does He inherit? All things (Rom. 8:32; Heb. 1:2)!

Christ inherits both earth and heaven (Matt. 28:18). There is an adoption that pertains to Israel (Rom. 9:4). Their primary inheritance is on the earth (Matt. 5:5; Jam. 2:5). There are three spheres of blessing in eternity: the new heaven, new earth, and new Jerusalem (Rev. 21:1-2). The inheritance of the Body of Christ is in heavenly places (Eph. 1:3, 9-11; 2:6-7; Col. 1:5). We will receive this inheritance with Christ when we are glorified together with Him (Col. 3:1-4; 1 Cor. 15:50-52; 2 Cor. 5:1).

When Paul said, "If so be" he was not making our inheritance conditional on suffering FOR Christ. The "if" is used in the sense of logic and argument, and not of condition or doubt. It is a Bible principle that suffering precedes glory. All believers suffer "WITH" Christ in this present life (v.18, 23, 26). Every member of the Body of Christ has an inheritance in Christ (Col. 1:12), but we may add weight to our glory through faithful suffering in the work of the ministry (2 Cor. 4:16-18; Col. 3:24; 2 Tim. 2:10-13). We will suffer loss at the judgment seat of Christ if we do not faithfully build according to the plans of the "wise masterbuilder" who laid the foundation for this present age (1 Cor. 3:10-15).

Being sons of God does not exempt us from suffering in this life. However, any suffering we go through is temporary and not worthy to be compared with the eternal glory that will be revealed in us when we are glorified together with Christ. The Bible principle is first suffering then glory.

The following passage demonstrates that all believers will suffer in this life, but nothing we go through will stop us from being glorified with Christ. ALL members of the Body of Christ will be glorified with Him because it is based on the predestinated purpose of God and not on our performance (vv.29-32).

The Sufferings of this Present Time

(18) For I reckon that the sufferings of this present time are not worthy to be compared with the glory which shall be revealed in us.
(19) For the earnest expectation of the creature waiteth for the manifestation of the sons of God.
(20) For the creature was made subject to vanity, not willingly, but by reason of him who hath subjected the same in hope,
(21) Because the creature itself also shall be delivered from the bondage of corruption into the glorious liberty of the children of God.
(22) For we know that the whole creation groaneth and travaileth in pain together until now.
(23) And not only they, but ourselves also, which have the firstfruits of the Spirit, even we ourselves groan within ourselves, waiting for the adoption, to wit, the redemption of our body.

Paul took it for granted that as long as we are in this fallen world in bodies of flesh we will deal with suffering. It is vital that we understand the issue of suffering according to the scripture, rightly divided. God made promises to Israel about health and wealth that He did not make to the Body of Christ (Duet. 7:12-15). Under the law covenant God promised Israel blessings for obedience and curses for disobedience. This is not how God is dealing with the Body of Christ under grace.

That we suffer does not mean that God is against us (Rom. 8:31). It is a fact of life for everyone who lives in this fallen world (Job 14:1). We will suffer even more if we believe and stand for the truth (Acts 14:22; Rom. 8:35-37; Phil. 1:29; 1 Thess. 3:3-4; 2 Tim. 3:11-12). Of course, we can also bring suffering upon ourselves and others through sinful choices (Gal. 6:7-8).

All our suffering will come to an eternal end when Christ comes for us to deliver us from this present evil world and to redeem our vile body. Christ purchased the redemption of our bodies on the cross, but He has not yet taken possession of all that He purchased. The Spirit of God has sealed us until the redemption of our body, and He is the firstfruits, or earnest (guarantee), that we will receive the glorified body that God has promised us (v.23; Eph. 1:13-14; 4:30; 1 Cor. 15:49-52). Any suffering that we endure in this temporal life is not worthy to be compared with the eternal glory that will be revealed in us. We must reckon (i.e., account) that to be so by faith not feelings (2 Cor. 4:16-18). We "groan within ourselves," not to merely get rid of this vile body, but to be clothed upon with our new body (2 Cor. 5:1-8).

Jesus Christ, the last Adam, redeemed what the first Adam ruined. Adam was the head of the old creation and when he fell the earth and its creatures were made subject to vanity (Ecc. 1:2) and brought under the bondage of corruption. A word that sums up life in this world is "PAIN." That God Himself has hope (v.20) proves that biblical hope is a certainty for He has no doubts. Christ will remove that bondage when He comes again to establish His righteous kingdom in the earth (Isa. 11:1-9; Matt. 19:28).

The Body of Christ will be caught up to heaven and glorified before the tribulation period. The earth will be partially delivered upon the second coming when God's earthly people, Israel, are delivered (Heb. 2:1-9). The glorified Body of Christ will be MANIFESTED to the world, although we will reign in heavenly places. There will be a connection between heaven and earth in the kingdom of heaven (Jn. 1:51). Death will not be destroyed until the great white throne judgment which will take place after the millennial reign (1 Cor. 15:26; Rev. 20:14). There will be no more corruption in the new earth.

Waiting in Hope

(24) For we are saved by hope: but hope that is seen is not hope: for what a man seeth, why doth he yet hope for?
(25) But if we hope for that we see not, then do we with patience wait for it.

How are we saved by hope? As we deal with the sufferings of this present time, we can be saved from discouragement, despair, and defeat by the Spirit of God making our hope real in our hearts as we believe what God has promised us (Rom. 15:13). Biblical hope is not a doubtful thing at all (v.20). Hope is an "earnest expectation" (Phil. 1:20) of something yet future. It concerns things we cannot see and that we must wait for. Hope is based on faith (2 Cor. 5:7; Heb. 11:1).

Christ has not yet taken possession of all that He redeemed on the cross. Our soul is redeemed (Rom. 3:24), but we are still waiting on the redemption of our body which will take place when Christ comes for us. The Spirit of God is the firstfruits, or earnest (guarantee), that we will receive the glorified body that God has promised us, and He seal us until the day of redemption (Eph. 1:13-14; 4:30). We will receive a glorified body like Christ (Phil. 3:20-21) that is fitted to reign with Christ eternal in the heavens (2 Cor. 5:1).

We have not seen the glorified Christ. We have not seen heaven. We have not seen the glory that He has promised us. But the hope that we should have in our hearts by faith makes it real and helps us to patiently wait for it (Rom. 5:1-5; 2 Thess. 3:5; Titus 2:13). This hope brings us great comfort (1 Thess. 4:13-18; 2 Thess. 2:16-17) and is great motivation for serving the Lord (Titus 2:11-15).

The Spirit Helps Our Infirmities

(26) Likewise the Spirit also helpeth our infirmities: for we know not what we should pray for as we ought: but the Spirit itself maketh intercession for us with groanings which cannot be uttered.
(27) And he that searcheth the hearts knoweth what is the mind of the Spirit, because he maketh intercession for the saints according to the will of God.
(28) And we know that all things work together for good to them that love God, to them who are the called according to his purpose.

As we patiently wait for the coming of Christ the ministry of the Spirit also helps our infirmities (i.e., weakness) by making intercession for us (i.e., praying for us). As we groan in pain (vv.22-23), the Spirit groans in sympathy (Isa. 63:9). We know that Paul is not talking about speaking in tongues, as some claim, because it is groanings which CANNOT be uttered. Christ, who searches the hearts (Rev. 2:23) and knows the mind of the Spirit, also makes intercession for us (v.27, 34). It is a comfort to know that the brethren pray for you, but nothing is more comforting than knowing that God is praying for you!

That we "know not what we should pray for as we ought" is proven by the fact we typically pray for God to keep us from suffering or to get us out of suffering. That is not the purpose of the Spirit's intercession. Our spiritual health is much more important than our physical health. God is more interested in changing us than He is in changing our circumstances. His grace is sufficient for all our infirmities (2 Cor. 12:7-10; Phil. 4:6-7).

God does not cause our suffering, but He can use it to teach us:
1) His word (Ps. 119:50, 71; Rom. 15:4)
2) Patience (Rom. 5:3)
3) To depend upon Him (2 Cor. 12:9)
4) To set our affections on things above (Col. 3:2)

We do not know how to pray as we ought, but the Spirit and Christ makes intercession for us according to the will of God and it is on that basis that one of the greatest promises in the Bible is given (v.28). This is an unconditional promise for ALL believers. ALL believers love God (although not always as we should) and ALL believers have been called according to His purpose. Paul did not say that all things are good, but that all things work together for good for those who are saved. Nothing we face in this life will stop God from fulfilling His purpose to conform us to the image of His Son (vv.29-30). There is also a sense in which the promise in verse 28 can be applied in this life (Gen. 50:20; Phil. 1:12).

For the lost, suffering is just suffering, and it will get much worse after death. For the saved, God uses temporal suffering for our spiritual and eternal good, and the best is yet to come!

We are Eternally Secure in Christ

(29) For whom he did foreknow, he also did predestinate to be conformed to the image of his Son, that he might be the firstborn among many brethren.
(30) Moreover whom he did predestinate, them he also called: and whom he called, them he also justified: and whom he justified, them he also glorified.
(31) What shall we then say to these things? If God be for us, who can be against us?
(32) He that spared not his own Son, but delivered him up for us all, how shall he not with him also freely give us all things?
(33) Who shall lay any thing to the charge of God's elect? It is God that justifieth.
(34) Who is he that condemneth? It is Christ that died, yea rather, that is risen again, who is even at the right hand of God, who also maketh intercession for us.
(35) Who shall separate us from the love of Christ? Shall tribulation, or distress, or persecution, or famine, or nakedness, or peril, or sword?

Study Notes

(36) As it is written, For thy sake we are killed all the day long; we are accounted as sheep for the slaughter.
(37) Nay, in all these things we are more than conquerors through him that loved us.
(38) For I am persuaded, that neither death, nor life, nor angels, nor principalities, nor powers, nor things present, nor things to come,
(39) Nor height, nor depth, nor any other creature, shall be able to separate us from the love of God, which is in Christ Jesus our Lord.

Those ignorant of the scripture think that if someone suffers the kind of things Paul mentioned in verse 35 it must mean God is against him. The oldest book in the world, Job, teaches that is not the case. Throughout church history believers have suffered all seven of the things in verse 35. The apostle Paul, who is our pattern, faced those things and his last inspired words before his execution were not words of defeat but of victory (2 Tim. 1:7-12, 4:6-8).

How are we "more than conquerors" in all these things? There is NOTHING that we can suffer in this life that can change the predestinated purpose that God has for us in Christ. Not only do we have the victory over all circumstances of life, but God can even use our suffering for our spiritual growth.

1) Foreknow – God knew before the foundation of the world all those who would choose to trust Christ. Election and predestination are based on the foreknowledge of God (1 Pet. 1:2). We will have more to say about election in chapter 9.

2) Predestinate – God purposed before the foundation of the world (Eph. 1:5, 11; 2 Tim. 1:9) that believers would be conformed to the image of His Son (firstborn is a position of authority, Col. 1:15-18). We will be perfectly conformed to His image upon the rapture (1 Cor. 15:49; Phil. 3:20-21), but the practical process of being changed should start in this life (2 Cor. 3:18; Phil. 3:12-14). The Bible never refers to anyone being predestinated to damnation.
3) Called – By the gospel (2 Thess. 2:14).
4) Justified – Declared righteous in Christ (Rom. 3:21-24).
5) Glorified – Spoken of in the past tense because the predestinated purpose of God is guaranteed (Rom. 8:23). Our glorification is not dependent upon our performance.

In the last nine verses Paul raises and answers seven questions to prove the eternal security of the believer.

1) What shall we say to these things? These five things prove that GOD IS FOR US and that no one can defeat His purpose for us.
2) If God be for us, who can be against us? The world, the flesh, and the devil are against us, but they cannot defeat us. God can take the things which seem to be against us (v.35) and work them together for our good (v.28).
3) How shall he not with him freely give us all things? Since Christ paid the full price of our redemption, He will fulfill all that He has promised us. Verse 32 proves that all members of the Body of Christ are joint-heirs with Christ (v.17).
4) Who shall lay anything to the charge of God's elect? Christ is the elect (Isa. 42:1) and we are chosen in Him

(Eph. 1:4). We do not get in Christ until we choose to trust Him as our Saviour.

5) Who is he that condemneth? No one, not even Satan, can lay anything to the charge of God's elect or condemn him (Rev. 12:10 is about tribulation saints). We are justified by His righteousness. For a member of the Body of Christ to be condemned would mean that the death, resurrection, and intercession of Christ are insufficient. Impossible!

6) Who shall separate us from the love of Christ? No one, not even ourselves (2 Tim. 2:13, 17-19).

7) Shall any of the seven things listed separate us? In verses 37-39 the apostle Paul answers the questions in verse 35. In verses 35-39 there are seventeen things listed (which covers everything) that cannot separate us from the love of God. What keeps us in the love of God is NOT our performance but our position as members of the Body of Christ. Our identity is in Him (Eph. 1:6).

Most denominations deny the doctrine of the eternal security of the believer because they do not rightly divide the word of truth (2 Tim. 2:15). They misuse passages that:
- Apply to some other dispensation (e.g., Ezek. 3:17-21; Matt. 24:13; Heb. 6:4-8)
- Do not apply to the Body of Christ (e.g., Rom. 11:13-24, the wild olive tree represents Gentiles as a whole)
- Do not apply to salvation (e.g., 1 Cor. 9:27, the context has to do with service, not salvation)

What Paul says to the Body of Christ in verses 35-39 is different from what Christ taught the Jewish kingdom saints (cf. John 15:1-10; Jude 21). In the coming tribulation period those that believe the gospel of the kingdom will have to face the seven things in verse 35 and some will take the mark of the beast to escape persecution and will thereby become separated from the love of God (the tribulation saints are not said to be "sealed" with the Spirit). That is one of the many reasons the Body of Christ is not going through the seventieth week of Daniel.

There are other passages that teach the eternal security of the Body of Christ (Eph. 1:13-14, 4:30; 2 Tim. 2:11-19). This great doctrine is a not "a license to sin" but a motive to serve the Lord with a heart full of gratitude and love.

We cannot lose salvation, but if we continually walk after the flesh we can lose our testimony, physical life, and eternal reward. It is possible for a believer who is alive in Christ to be walking as though they are still dead (Rom. 8:13; Eph. 5:14; 1 Tim. 5:6).

Romans 9

The emphasis in the first eight chapters of Romans was on the doctrine of salvation by the faith of Christ that is offered freely to all condemned sinners, both Jews and Gentiles for there is no difference in this present age of grace. The emphasis in the last five chapters (12-16) will be on applying that doctrine to our practical walk. In between stands a parenthetical passage of three chapters (9-11) in which there is a dispensational emphasis as Paul answers questions concerning God's dealings with Israel. In light of the doctrine set forth in the first eight chapters, the question naturally arises, "Hath God cast away His people?" (Rom. 11:1) This section is about Israel, but Paul is speaking to the Gentiles (Rom. 11:13).

In the previous passage Paul argued that the believer is secure and that nothing can defeat God's predestinated purpose for us in Christ. But someone might ask, "What about the Jews? They were chosen by God and given covenants and yet you say there is no longer any difference between them and the Gentiles. Will God fail to keep His promises to Israel? If God was not faithful to the Jews, how can we be sure that He will be faithful to the Body of Christ?"

In this section Paul has something to say about Israel's
- Past Election (Rom. 9)
- Present Rejection (Rom. 10)
- Future Salvation (Rom. 11)

I. The Problem (vv.1-5) – Has God's word failed concerning Israel?
II. The Explanation (vv.6-13) – They are not all Israel, which are of Israel.
III. Objections Refuted (vv.14-24) – God is not obligated to save every Israelite.
IV. Scriptural Proof (vv.25-29) – God has a remnant.
V. The Conclusion (vv.30-33) – Israel fell because of unbelief.

The Problem

(1) I say the truth in Christ, I lie not, my conscience also bearing me witness in the Holy Ghost,
(2) That I have great heaviness and continual sorrow in my heart.
(3) For I could wish that myself were accursed from Christ for my brethren, my kinsmen according to the flesh:
(4) Who are Israelites; to whom pertaineth the adoption, and the glory, and the covenants, and the giving of the law, and the service of God, and the promises;
(5) Whose are the fathers, and of whom as concerning the flesh Christ came, who is over all, God blessed for ever. Amen.

In the opening passage of this section Paul expressed his deep burden for the unbelieving Jews (Rom. 10:1). Paul had been falsely accused of being a traitor to his own brethren and of being against Israel, but he solemnly confirmed his burden for them by expressing with the full awareness that he was speaking in Christ with his conscience and the Holy Ghost bearing witness to the truth of his testimony (2 Cor. 13:1).

The same man that said, "Rejoice in the Lord alway: and again I say, Rejoice" also said "I have continual sorrow in my heart." That is one of the paradoxes of the Christian life (2 Cor. 6:10).

What Paul said in verse 3 is so unbelievable that we would assume he was lying if he was not speaking by inspiration of God. Paul knew that he could not be accursed from Christ (Rom. 8:35-39) so he said he "COULD WISH" it if it meant the salvation of Israel. This expresses the love of Christ. Christ was made a curse for us that we might be redeemed (Gal. 3:13). The only other man who came close having such a burden for Israel was Moses (Ex. 32:31-32).

Paul summarized the privileges of Israel (Rom. 3:1-2) to prove that God still has a purpose for them. Notice that he did not say, "to whom pertained in the past."

1) Adoption (Ex. 4:22; Hos. 1:10) – Full placement as an adult son
2) Glory (Ex. 29:43; Ezek. 43:1-5) – The presence of God
3) Covenants –Israel is God's covenant people (cf. Eph. 2:12)
4) Giving of the law (Ps. 147:19-20)
5) Service of God (Ex. 19:5-6; Heb. 9:1, 6) – As a kingdom of priests
6) The promises (Rom. 15:8)
7) The fathers – Abraham, Isaac, Jacob, David
8) Of whom Christ came – He is the seed of David, of tribe of Judah (the last part of v.5 declares the deity of Christ)

In light of their great privileges, how do we explain their present condition (1 Thess. 2:14-16)?

The Explanation

(6) Not as though the word of God hath taken none effect. For they are not all Israel, which are of Israel:

(7) Neither, because they are the seed of Abraham, are they all children: but, In Isaac shall thy seed be called.

(8) That is, They which are the children of the flesh, these are not the children of God: but the children of the promise are counted for the seed.

(9) For this is the word of promise, At this time will I come, and Sara shall have a son.

(10) And not only this; but when Rebecca also had conceived by one, even by our father Isaac;

(11) (For the children being not yet born, neither having done any good or evil, that the purpose of God according to election might stand, not of works, but of him that calleth;)

(12) It was said unto her, The elder shall serve the younger.

(13) As it is written, Jacob have I loved, but Esau have I hated.

The word of God is effectual (Isa. 55:10-11; Rom. 3:1-4; 1 Thess. 2:13; Heb. 4:1-2, 12). Therefore, the problem lies with man. Unbelieving Israel was responsible for rejecting the word of God. Just being of the physical seed of Abraham (of the flesh) does not guarantee all that God promised. They had to be of the promised seed AND believe God as Abraham did (Matt. 3:7-10; Jn. 8:37-39; Rom. 2:28-29; Gal. 6:16).

The election God made concerning Isaac's children was not of Jacob to salvation and Esau to damnation. It was simply that the elder should serve the younger (Gen. 25:21-23). It had to do with the covenants and promises concerning Israel. That God said He hated Esau does not mean he was predestinated to damnation. The word "hate" can be used in the comparative sense of being less loved (Gen. 29:30-31; Lk. 14:26). When did God say He hated Esau? Not before the foundation of the world, but after Esau sold his birthright and his descendants persecuted Israel (Mal. 1:1-4).

Calvinists take this chapter out of context and imagine that it supports their theology. They are, for the most part, anti-dispensational in how they approach the Bible. They think the church is spiritual Israel and that every time the word "election" shows up it is talking about individual salvation.

The five major points of Calvinism can be summarized by the acronym **TULIP**. They begin with a wrong premise and that leads them to wrong conclusions.

1) **Total Depravity** – They believe that through the fall of Adam all who are born into this world are depraved to the point of being incapable of responding to God in faith.

While the flesh is certainly corrupt and condemned (Rom. 3:1-20), the Bible does not teach that a lost person cannot choose to believe the word of God. They should call it "Total Inability." Faith is not a work (Rom. 4:5)!

2) **Unconditional Election** – They believe that man is unable to respond to God; therefore, in eternity past God elected and predestinated certain people to salvation. Election and predestination are unconditional; they are

not based on man's response because man is unable to respond, nor does he want to.

In the Bible there are various individuals and groups that are said to be elect, and it always has to do with service, not salvation. Predestination concerns God's purpose for those who choose to trust Christ as their Saviour. Election and predestination are based on God's foreknowledge (Rom. 8:29; 1 Pet. 1:2).

3) **Limited Atonement** – They believe that because God determined that certain ones should be saved, He determined that Christ should die for the elect alone. All whom God has elected and for whom Christ died will be saved.

Christ died for all that are dead in sin (2 Cor. 5:14-15). He tasted death for EVERY man (Heb. 2:9). He is the Saviour of all men, specially of those that believe (1 Tim. 4:10).

4) **Irresistible Grace** – They believe that God draws those whom he elected to Himself through irresistible grace. God makes man willing to come to Him. When God calls, man responds.

There are examples in the Bible of men resisting the Holy Ghost (Acts 7:51; 24:24-25; 26:28).

5) **Perseverance of the Saints** – They believe that the precise ones God has elected and drawn to Himself through the Holy Spirit will persevere in faith. None

whom God has elected will be lost; they are eternally secure.

The Body of Christ certainly has eternal security, but Calvinists sound more like Armenians on this point because they believe election must be proven by a lifetime of good WORKS.

You don't have to be a Calvinist or an Armenian. Be a Bible-believer!

The Objections

(14) What shall we say then? Is there unrighteousness with God? God forbid.
(15) For he saith to Moses, I will have mercy on whom I will have mercy, and I will have compassion on whom I will have compassion.
(16) So then it is not of him that willeth, nor of him that runneth, but of God that sheweth mercy.

Paul anticipated that a natural man, who cannot understand the ways of God (1 Cor. 2:14), would claim there was unrighteous with God. Paul's answer was, "God forbid." The righteous Lord has the right to have mercy and compassion on whomever He will, even the Gentiles (Rom. 11:32). In the context of when God told Moses "I will have mercy on whom I will have mercy, and I will have compassion on whom I will have compassion" (Ex. 33:19), He had every right to destroy the children of Israel for their idolatry but chose instead to spare them. No man can force God by his will or actions to have mercy or compassion on him apart from the conditions that God has chosen to show mercy and compassion.

Do you want God to show mercy and compassion to you as a condemned sinner? Then CHOOSE to trust Christ as your Saviour! Paul did NOT say that God foreordained that He would not have mercy or compassion on certain individuals. The Lord did not say, "I will condemn whom I will condemn, and I will reprobate to eternal damnation whom I will reprobate."

(17) For the scripture saith unto Pharaoh, Even for this same purpose have I raised thee up, that I might shew my power in thee, and that my name might be declared throughout all the earth.
(18) Therefore hath he mercy on whom he will have mercy, and whom he will he hardeneth.

God spoke to Pharaoh, but Paul said, "the scripture saith to Pharaoh" because the scripture is the living word of God (Gal. 3:8, 22). This is an example of an inspired translation. God spoke through Moses in Hebrew, and Aaron translated it to Pharaoh in Egyptian, it was recorded in Hebrew, and Paul wrote it in Greek and called it SCRIPTURE (2 Tim. 3:16). The King James Bible is the inspired scripture preserved in English.

God did not cause Pharaoh to be the evil man that he was, but he used him to demonstrate His power over the idols of Egypt that the world might know that He is the true and living God. The Lord hardened Pharaoh AFTER he first rejected the word of God (Ex. 4:21; 5:1-2; 8:15).

A note in the Old Scofield Reference Bible (pg. 75) says, "In the face of the righteous demand of Jehovah and of the tremendous attestations by miracle that He was indeed God, and that Moses and Aaron were His representatives, Pharaoh "hardened his heart." Instrumentally God hardened Pharaoh's heart by forcing him to an issue against which he hardened his own heart in refusal. Light rejected, rightful obedience refused, inevitably hardens conscience and heart."

(19) Thou wilt say then unto me, Why doth he yet find fault? For who hath resisted his will?
(20) Nay but, O man, who art thou that repliest against God? Shall the thing formed say to him that formed it, Why hast thou made me thus?
(21) Hath not the potter power over the clay, of the same lump to make one vessel unto honour, and another unto dishonour?
(22) What if God, willing to shew his wrath, and to make his power known, endured with much longsuffering the vessels of wrath fitted to destruction:
(23) And that he might make known the riches of his glory on the vessels of mercy, which he had afore prepared unto glory,
(24) Even us, whom he hath called, not of the Jews only, but also of the Gentiles?

Paul brings up the illustration of the potter and the clay, which has to do with God's dealings with His earthly people Israel, in refuting the objections of the unbelieving Jews. He anticipated that the unbelieving Jews (Rom. 2:1-5) would reply that they had not resisted God's will and that they were in the condition that God forced upon them (Isa. 63:17). Paul rebuked such a question coming from a finite man to an infinite God. Israel certainly had resisted God's will (Acts 7:51).

Within the "same lump" of clay (Israel) there are vessels of honor and dishonor (v.6). How God formed them and what He did with them was based on *their response to His word* (Isa. 29:13-16; 45:9-11; 64:6-9; Jer. 18:1-10; 19:10-13). When did God make vessels of wrath fit for destruction? Before the foundation of the world? No, it was AFTER they rejected His word. When did He prepare the vessels of mercy? It was AFTER they believed His word. Paul himself had been a vessel of wrath that became a vessel of mercy ("chosen vessel" for service).

In the professing church there are also vessels of honor and dishonor. Which one we are is also based upon our response to the word of God (2 Tim. 2:20-21).

In this present age God is calling Jews and Gentiles through Paul's gospel (2 Thess. 2:14), but we must choose to respond by faith.

The Scriptural Proof

(25) As he saith also in Osee, I will call them my people, which were not my people; and her beloved, which was not beloved.
(26) And it shall come to pass, that in the place where it was said unto them, Ye are not my people; there shall they be called the children of the living God.
(27) Esaias also crieth concerning Israel, Though the number of the children of Israel be as the sand of the sea, a remnant shall be saved:
(28) For he will finish the work, and cut it short in righteousness: because a short work will the Lord make upon the earth.

(29) And as Esaias said before, Except the Lord of Sabaoth had left us a seed, we had been as Sodoma, and been made like unto Gomorrha.

The OT prophets predicted the fall of Israel and the salvation of a believing remnant. Paul quoted from Hosea (1:10; 2:23) and Isaiah (1:9; 10:22-23) to prove his point. The quotes are about a believing remnant in Israel, the little flock (1 Pet. 2:6-10), not the Body of Christ which was a mystery hid from the prophets. However, Paul applied the principle of those prophecies to his Acts ministry (v.24) in which a remnant in Israel became members of the Body of Christ (Rom. 11:5-6). That Paul sometimes *applied* the principle of a prophecy to his ministry (when dealing with the Jews) does not mean he had not yet received the mystery or that he thought his ministry was the fulfillment of it (Acts 13:47).

The Conclusion

(30) What shall we say then? That the Gentiles, which followed not after righteousness, have attained to righteousness, even the righteousness which is of faith.
(31) But Israel, which followed after the law of righteousness, hath not attained to the law of righteousness.
(32) Wherefore? Because they sought it not by faith, but as it were by the works of the law. For they stumbled at that stumblingstone;
(33) As it is written, Behold, I lay in Sion a stumblingstone and rock of offence: and whosoever believeth on him shall not be ashamed.

What an indictment against unbelieving Israel that Gentiles, who were far off from God, were being saved and made righteous in Christ (Rom. 3:20-22) while they stumbled over their own Messiah! Paul did not say they stumbled because they were predestinated to do so, but because they chose to trust in their own works instead of believing on Christ (Rom. 10:1-4).

Christ crucified is a stumbling block to the self-righteous Jews (1 Cor. 1:23). The stone which the builders (religious leaders) rejected (Ps. 118:22) and stumbled over (Isa. 8:14; 28:16) is the chief corner stone of salvation. But there was a believing remnant in Israel, the little flock, that will get the kingdom (Matt. 21:33-46). That is not the same remnant of Jews that believed Paul's gospel and were baptized into the Body of Christ.

Romans 10

In the last chapter Paul expressed his deep burden for unbelieving Israel and showed how that despite being God's chosen nation they had willfully rejected Him. Yet there was a remnant that believed on Christ. In this chapter, he will prove that unbelieving Israel was responsible for the condition they were in. The "righteousness which is of faith" (Rom. 9:30; 10:6) was available to them (Rom. 10:6-8), offered to them (Rom. 10:12-13), but rejected by them (Rom. 10:16, 21).

(1) Brethren, my heart's desire and prayer to God for Israel is, that they might be saved.

Because of his ministry to the Gentiles, Paul had been accused of being against Israel, but nothing was further from the truth! He begins each chapter in this section (Rom. 9-11) declaring his burden and desire to see his unbelieving brethren saved. By the way, if they were predestinated to damnation, what would be the point in praying for them? We pray about what is on our heart.

Paul was praying for their salvation *in this present age of grace*. There was no need for him to pray for Israel to be saved as a nation at the second coming of Christ, because it is guaranteed by the word prophecy (Rom. 11:26). There are several things that Paul said in this passage that prove he is talking about salvation in this present age (Rom. 10:4, 8, 12).

(2) For I bear them record that they have a zeal of God, but not according to knowledge.

Paul knew all about their religious zeal because he had been just like them (Gal. 1:13-14). They were zealous for the traditions of men and not for the truth of God. Had they truly loved the word of God they would have recognized their own Messiah of whom their scriptures prophesied. Knowledge without zeal won't accomplish much, but zeal without knowledge is dangerous! To have both is an important balance in serving God.

(3) For they being ignorant of God's righteousness, and going about to establish their own righteousness, have not submitted themselves unto the righteousness of God.

They were zealous in going about to establish their own righteousness which proved their absolute ignorance of God's righteousness. In time past God required a man under the law to have the righteousness which is of the law (Deut. 6:24-25; Lk. 1:5-6), but he was not to trust in his own righteousness (Lk. 18:9-14). But now, in this present age, the righteousness of God which is by faith of Jesus Christ has been revealed (Rom. 3:19-24; Phil. 3:1-9). Like unbelieving Israel, the religious world today is busy trying to establish their own righteousness (Isa. 64:6; Phil. 3:8) instead of submitting to the righteousness of God.

(4) For Christ *is* the end of the law for righteousness to every one that believeth.

What is meant by "the end of the law?" Is Christ the goal of the law or the termination of the law? Both are true. The condemnation of the law is designed to point sinners to Christ for justification (Gal. 3:24-25). Being made righteous in Christ, we are dead to the law (Rom. 7:4), delivered from the law (Rom. 7:6), and not under the law (Rom. 6:14).

(5) For Moses describeth the righteousness which is of the law, That the man which doeth those things shall live by them.

In this section (Rom. 9-11) Paul quotes or alludes to many OT scriptures because he is dealing with Israel in the context. The righteousness of the law was by faith, but it was faith proven by works (Lev. 18:5). They had to do all the law, all the time, and when they failed, they had to bring the required sacrifice by faith with a repentant heart.

(6) But the righteousness which is of faith speaketh on this wise, Say not in thine heart, Who shall ascend into heaven? (that is, to bring Christ down *from above:*)
(7) Or, Who shall descend into the deep? (that is, to bring up Christ again from the dead.)
(8) But what saith it? The word is nigh thee, *even* in thy mouth, and in thy heart: that is, the word of faith, which we preach;

In contrast with "the righteousness which is of the law," a sinner does not have to do anything to receive "the righteousness which is of faith" but simply BELIEVE (Rom. 10:4, 10). Christ has already come down from heaven to die for our sins and rise again from the dead. It is a finished work offered freely to those who believe (Rom. 3:20-24). Paul alluded to a passage in the law (Deut. 30:11-14) to show that God has been faithful to make His revelation known to His people. Notice how Paul, by inspiration, exchanged "Christ" for the "commandment." Just as God had made His commandment known to Israel, He has now made the righteousness of Christ known and available for them to receive through Paul's Acts ministry in which he went "to the Jew first" (Rom. 1:16). Paul did not preach the gospel of the kingdom to the Jews in the Acts period (v.8; Acts 13:38-39).

(9) That if thou shalt confess with thy mouth the Lord Jesus, and shalt believe in thine heart that God hath raised him from the dead, thou shalt be saved.
(10) For with the heart man believeth unto righteousness; and with the mouth confession is made unto salvation.
(11) For the scripture saith, Whosoever believeth on him shall not be ashamed.
(12) For there is no difference between the Jew and the Greek: for the same Lord over all is rich unto all that call upon him.
(13) For whosoever shall call upon the name of the Lord shall be saved.

This has become a controversial passage because most professing Christians don't seem to understand it. Many use it to support the "sinner's prayer" approach to evangelism. They claim that a sinner must vocally call upon the Lord to be saved, and they emphasize prayer over faith. Some dispensationalists, seeing the error of this approach, claim that this passage is only for Israel and has no application in this present age of grace. The apostle Paul was certainly talking about Israel in the context, but he was speaking to the Gentiles (Rom. 11:13). Besides, in the context Paul is talking about the need for Israel in this present age to receive the righteousness which is by faith.

Paul is not talking about the confession required under the gospel of the kingdom (Matt. 10:32-33) in this passage. The context is clearly different. Paul says nothing in this passage about confessing Christ before men or being denied before the Father if we fail to do so. In the context, Paul is not talking about the gospel of the kingdom, but "the word of faith, which we preach." He did not preach the gospel of the kingdom to Israel in his Acts ministry (Gal. 1:6-12). There was a remnant of Jews that believed Paul's gospel and were baptized into the Body of Christ (Rom. 11:5-6). Paul preached one message of salvation throughout his entire ministry.

This passage does not teach that we must literally confess with our physical mouth to be saved. That would contradict Paul's emphasis upon FAITH as the only condition for salvation, which was already established in the doctrinal section of this epistle. And what about mutes? They cannot confess anything audibly. When he said to believe in our heart, he did not mean that we must believe with our literal blood pump. He is referring to confession in the sense of heartfelt acknowledgement.

Confession is not merely saying words. Devils said that Jesus was the the Son of God (Mk. 5:7-8), but they did not confess Him (1 Jn. 4:1-2, 15). We can call upon God from the heart without saying words. Besides, confession means nothing without believing. It is with the HEART we believe unto righteousness. Believing on Christ for salvation is not merely a mental assent, but a heartfelt trust (Eph. 1:13). It is good to publicly confess Christ. What is in our heart will come out of our mouth (Rom. 10:11; Matt. 12:34; 2 Cor. 4:13). But we do not have to confess Christ publicly *to be saved.*

Some claim that prayer is a work and that asking Christ to save you means that you did not believe the gospel. Prayer can be a spiritual work in the Christian life (Col. 4:12) but saying a simple prayer from a believing heart that is trusting the finished work of Christ is not a work. The issue in salvation is not prayer, but faith. It is wrong to tell people that they must pray to be saved, but it is also wrong to tell people that they are not saved if they prayed when they believed the gospel. Do you really think that if a sinner prays when they trust Christ as their Saviour that God will not save them?

What Paul said in verse 12 is a great dispensational truth for this present age, which proves this passage is not about Israel's future salvation. There is no difference between Jews and Gentiles in sin (Rom. 3:22) or salvation. That Paul quoted from Joel 2:32 concerning salvation in the future day of the Lord does not prove that is what this passage is about. He was obviously making a spiritual application.

(14) How then shall they call on him in whom they have not believed? and how shall they believe in him of whom they have not heard? and how shall they hear without a preacher?
(15) And how shall they preach, except they be sent? as it is written, How beautiful are the feet of them that preach the gospel of peace, and bring glad tidings of good things!

Israel could have called on the Lord because God did indeed send preachers to them with a message of peace (Isa. 52:7; defines gospel as good tidings, Nah. 1:15). He sent them the greatest preacher of all, His own Son (Acts 10:36-38). Christ trained and sent His twelve apostles to Israel with the gospel of the kingdom (Jn. 20:21). Israel rejected and crucified Christ, but they were given an opportunity to repent and a renewed offer of the kingdom in the book of Acts (Acts 10:39-43). They rejected the witness of the Holy Ghost through the apostles. In amazing longsuffering God also sent Paul to the Jew first during the Acts period with the gospel of Christ which is a message of peace to the individual sinner (Eph. 6:15).

The order in how sinners come to call upon the Lord for salvation is given in reverse in vv.14-15 (note "how"):
1) They CALL because
2) They BELIEVE because
3) They HEARD because
4) Of a PREACHER who was
5) SENT by God

God has done His part in sending preachers (2 Cor. 5:17-20). The problem is that so many of His people are not doing their part to carry the gospel to the lost. We must use our feet to take it to them (Eph. 6:15).

(16) But they have not all obeyed the gospel. For Esaias saith, Lord, who hath believed our report?
(17) So then faith *cometh* by hearing, and hearing by the word of God.
(18) But I say, Have they not heard? Yes verily, their sound went into all the earth, and their words unto the ends of the world.

That Israel would reject Christ was prophesied by Isaiah. They were also now rejecting the gospel of Christ. The only way to obey the gospel of Christ is to believe it ("obedience of faith,"

Rom. 16:26). Faith is believing the word of God (v.17; Rom. 4:3-5).

In verse 18 Paul begins to anticipate and answer objections. They heard the word of God and therefore they could have believed the message. The gospel was going out to the world. The whole world has some light (Ps. 19:1-7).

(19) But I say, Did not Israel know? First Moses saith, I will provoke you to jealousy by *them that are* no people, *and* by a foolish nation I will anger you.
(20) But Esaias is very bold, and saith, I was found of them that sought me not; I was made manifest unto them that asked not after me.
(21) But to Israel he saith, All day long I have stretched forth my hands unto a disobedient and gainsaying people.

Paul is not referring to the Gentiles in verse 19. How can the nations be called, "a foolish nation" (Deut. 32:21)? God did use the Gentiles to provoke Israel to jealousy (Rom. 11:11), but before He did that, He was provoking unbelieving Israel with the little flock (Matt. 21:33-46; Lk. 12:32). They were considered "no people" and a "foolish nation" because of their small number and the fact they were made up primarily of common people. Christ poured out His Spirit on them as they preached to Israel, and they brought forth the fruits of the kingdom of God.

Neither is Paul referring to the Gentiles in verses 20-21. Christ sent the little flock to preach to the very ones that crucified Him and wanted nothing to do with Him, and they stubbornly persisted in their rejection of Him (Isa. 65:1-7). Paul himself had been one of those, but he was saved by exceeding abundant grace. In amazing longsuffering, God also sent Paul to get a remnant out of Israel before He set them aside as a nation (Rom. 11:1-6). Israel fell in Acts 7 (when they stoned Stephen who was filled with the Holy Ghost), but there was a transition period until Acts 28. This remnant explains certain things about Paul's ministry during the book of Acts. Israel was a disobedient and gainsaying people, yet Paul still had a heart to reach them (Rom. 10:1).

Romans 11

In the previous chapter the apostle Paul proved that unbelieving Israel was responsible for rejecting God's righteousness. In this chapter he explains that although the majority in Israel were spiritually blinded, a remnant out of Israel was being saved. The blindness of Israel was partial, and it is not permanent. There is coming a day, after this present age, when Israel will be saved as a nation (vv.25-27).

This chapter refutes "Replacement Theology" which claims the church replaced the nation of Israel. We are living in a parenthetical mystery age that interrupted God's prophetic dealings with Israel. The Body of Christ is a "new creature," not spiritual Israel (Gal. 6:15-16). God will literally fulfill all of the promises He made to the nation of Israel (Rom. 9:4-5).

In this chapter Paul explains the dispensational changes in God's dealings with Israel and the Gentiles in this present age. He demonstrates how that through Israel's fall the Gentiles have now been brought into a place of blessing. This is completely different from what we find in prophecy. The prophets spoke of God blessing the Gentiles through Israel's RISE, not through their FALL. Paul calls this a mystery (v.25) and informs us that it is not a permanent arrangement. God will resume His previous dealings with Israel and fulfill all His promises to them.

In the meantime, during Paul's ministry in the Acts period, God was using His blessings on the Gentiles to provoke Israel to jealousy which resulted in some of them being saved. The chapter closes with praise to God for His great wisdom in how He has worked all of this out.

A Remnant

(1) I say then, Hath God cast away his people? God forbid. For I also am an Israelite, of the seed of Abraham, of the tribe of Benjamin.
(2) God hath not cast away his people which he foreknew. Wot ye not what the scripture saith of Elias? how he maketh intercession to God against Israel, saying,

In this same chapter Paul said that God has not cast away His people but then he referred to the casting away of Israel (v.15). How can both be true? There is a difference between the true Israel of God and unbelieving Israel (Rom. 9:6). God foreknew the Jews who would believe, and they were not cast away. Paul himself was proof that not all of Israel was in unbelief.

(2) God hath not cast away his people which he foreknew. Wot ye not what the scripture saith of Elias? how he maketh intercession to God against Israel, saying,
(3) Lord, they have killed thy prophets, and digged down thine altars; and I am left alone, and they seek my life.
(4) But what saith the answer of God unto him? I have reserved to myself seven thousand men, who have not bowed the knee to the image of Baal.
(5) Even so then at this present time also there is a remnant according to the election of grace.

(6) And if by grace, then is it no more of works: otherwise grace is no more grace. But if it be of works, then is it no more grace: otherwise work is no more work.

Under the law Elijah made intercession *against* Israel, but under grace Paul made intercession *for* them (Rom. 10:1). A "remnant" is the residue, or that which remains (Zeph. 2:9). God had a believing remnant in Israel's history, and He will have a remnant in the future tribulation period. The little flock of believing Israel was a remnant that will inherit the kingdom (Rom. 9:25-29).

There was also another remnant of Israel that could not be part of that little flock because they blasphemed the Holy Ghost (Matt. 12:31-32), but they could be saved by grace through Paul's gospel and be put into the Body of Christ. In amazing longsuffering, God used Paul's ministry to get a remnant out of Israel before He set them aside as a nation. Israel fell in Acts 7 when they stoned Stephen (who preached to them filled with the Holy Ghost) but there was a transition until Acts 28. During this transition Paul went to the Jew first (Rom. 1:16). This explains certain things about Paul's ministry during the book of Acts. For example, why would the same apostle who said that we are not under the law put himself under a Jewish vow (Acts 18:18)? You will find his explanation in 1 Corinthians 9:19-20.

The "election of grace" does not refer to a select few that God unconditionally and arbitrarily chose to salvation. The Body of Christ was chosen "in Him" before the foundation of the world (Eph. 1:4). How did we get in Him? By believing the gospel of the grace of God (Eph. 1:12-13). God foreknew all who would believe the gospel and He called us by the gospel (Rom. 8:29-30; 2 Thess. 2:13-14).

Salvation by grace cannot be mixed with works. Paul said that salvation in this age is "no more of works," "not of works" (Eph. 2:9), and "not by works" (Titus 3:5). To add works to the gospel of Christ is to pervert it (Gal. 1:6-12).

Paul said that it was "no more of works" because in times past God did require works to prove faith (Rom. 10:5). The gospel of the kingdom required water baptism and bringing forth fruits meet for repentance (Matt. 3:7-10). God is gracious in every age but there is a difference between Noah finding grace (i.e., favor) in the eyes of the Lord because he was a just man and perfect in his generations (Gen. 6:8-9) and Christ saving Saul of Tarsus by exceeding abundant grace when he was on his way to persecute His people (1 Tim. 1:13-16). Paul gradually received revelations, but he could not have received the gospel gradually (it is either grace or it is not), which proves he did not preach the gospel of the kingdom during his ministry in Acts as some claim.

(7) What then? Israel hath not obtained that which he seeketh for; but the election hath obtained it, and the rest were blinded
(8) (According as it is written, God hath given them the spirit of slumber, eyes that they should not see, and ears that they should not hear;) unto this day.
(9) And David saith, Let their table be made a snare, and a trap, and a stumblingblock, and a recompence unto them:
(10) Let their eyes be darkened, that they may not see, and bow down their back alway.

Unbelieving Israel sought after righteousness but did not obtain it (Rom. 9:30-10:4). The remnant according to the election of grace obtained righteousness in Christ and the rest of Israel was blinded (i.e., spiritually blinded to God's righteousness and truth). Paul quoted Isaiah (29:10) and David (Ps. 69:20-24, prophecy of the rejection of Christ) concerning Israel's blindness. Their blindness was the **result** of their unbelief and not the **reason** for it. Their "table" (symbol of their blessings) was made a snare to them because the word of God is a two-edged sword that can save or condemn based on the response of those who hear It.

The Fall of Israel

(11) I say then, Have they stumbled that they should fall? God forbid: but rather through their fall salvation is come unto the Gentiles, for to provoke them to jealousy.
(12) Now if the fall of them be the riches of the world, and the diminishing of them the riches of the Gentiles; how much more their fulness?
(13) For I speak to you Gentiles, inasmuch as I am the apostle of the Gentiles, I magnify mine office:
(14) If by any means I may provoke to emulation them which are my flesh, and might save some of them.
(15) For if the casting away of them be the reconciling of the world, what shall the receiving of them be, but life from the dead?

Paul's main point is that the stumbling, fall, diminishing, and casting away of Israel did not defeat God's purpose to bless the nations, and neither is it permanent.

Yes, they stumbled and fell but through their fall God was now saving Gentiles, and through that He was provoking them to jealousy so that individual Jews might come to Him for salvation.

Yes, they were being diminished while the Gentiles were receiving the riches of God's blessings, but how much more will the nations of world be blessed when Israel enjoys the fullness that God has promised them (e.g., Ps. 67).

Yes, they were being cast away, but they will yet be received. When God receives them there will be life from the dead. The resurrection of Israel as a nation (Ezek. 37) will have a life-giving impact on the world (Matt. 19:28).

Man's failure cannot defeat God's good purpose. Joseph's brethren failed when they moved with envy sold him into slavery. They thought evil against him, but God meant it unto good (Gen. 50:20). That pictures how Israel thought evil against Christ, but God meant it unto good.

Notice the four terms that describe unbelieving Israel's condition.

1) Stumbled – Rejection of Christ (Rom. 9:31-33). They received a renewed offer because of Christ's intercession (Lk. 23:34).
2) Fall – Rejection of the Holy Ghost (Matt. 12:31-32; Acts 7:51-60).
3) Diminishing – During the transition period (Acts 8-28).
4) Casting away – God rejected them because they rejected Him (Father, Son, and Spirit).

This passage refutes Acts 28 Dispensationalism (the false idea that the Body of Christ did not start until after Acts 28) because it proves Israel fell before Paul wrote Romans at the time of Acts 20. The OT prophets spoke of the blindness of Israel, but it was a mystery that through their fall salvation would come unto the Gentiles (v.25). According to prophecy, Gentiles were to be blessed through Israel's RISE (Isa. 60:1-3). In this age Gentiles are being saved through Israel's FALL, there is now no difference between Jew and Gentile, and all believers are in one spiritual Body (1 Cor. 12:13).

Most modern versions change verse 13 to say, "AN apostle of the Gentiles." It is strange that so many professing Christians minimize what God magnifies. God magnified His word above all His name (Ps. 138:2), yet many cast doubt on it and try to correct it. The word of God emphasizes the fact that Paul's apostleship was distinct from the twelve apostles (see Gal. 1-2). He was God chosen vessel to preach the unsearchable riches of Christ among the Gentiles. Although Paul was not the only apostle sent to the Gentiles (Barnabas, Acts 14:14) he was "THE apostle to the Gentiles." One apostle is a fitting representative of the one Body of Christ. Paul was a free-born Roman citizen (Acts 22:25-28) but also a Hebrew of the Hebrews (Phil. 3:5).

Paul magnified his office as the apostle to the Gentiles (signs and wonders, Rom. 15:16-19) in an effort to provoke his Jewish brethren to emulation (an attempt to equal or excel others in that which is praiseworthy) that some of them might be saved. This provoking ministry helps us understand some things about Paul's ministry in the Acts period.

What Paul said in verse 15 proves the Body of Christ did not begin in early Acts when Israel was given a renewed offer of the kingdom. The fact that we are reconciled "BY THE CROSS" (Eph. 2:16) doesn't mean that the offer of reconciliation went out to all men immediately after the cross. It was AFTER the fall and casting away of unbelieving Israel that God began to reconcile both Jews and Gentiles into one Body.

The Olive Tree

(16) For if the firstfruit be holy, the lump is also holy: and if the root be holy, so are the branches.

The "firstfruit" and "root" refer to the Jewish fathers (v.28). If God set them apart ("holy") and gave them and their seed promises of great blessings, it is guaranteed that which springs from them ("lump" and "branches") will also be set apart to inherit those blessings. That SOME of the branches are broken off does not destroy the root of the tree.

(17) And if some of the branches be broken off, and thou, being a wild olive tree, wert graffed in among them, and with them partakest of the root and fatness of the olive tree;
(18) Boast not against the branches. But if thou boast, thou bearest not the root, but the root thee.
(19) Thou wilt say then, The branches were broken off, that I might be graffed in.
(20) Well; because of unbelief they were broken off, and thou standest by faith. Be not highminded, but fear:
(21) For if God spared not the natural branches, take heed lest he also spare not thee.

(22) Behold therefore the goodness and severity of God: on them which fell, severity; but toward thee, goodness, if thou continue in his goodness: otherwise thou also shalt be cut off.
(23) And they also, if they abide not still in unbelief, shall be graffed in: for God is able to graff them in again.
(24) For if thou wert cut out of the olive tree which is wild by nature, and wert graffed contrary to nature into a good olive tree: how much more shall these, which be the natural branches, be graffed into their own olive tree?

This is one of the most misunderstood passages in the Bible and false teaching is the result. For example, those who deny the doctrine of eternal security claim this passage teaches believers can lose salvation. Paul is not talking about the salvation of individual members of the Body of Christ in the context. He is certainly not contradicting what he already taught when he was talking about that (Rom. 8:35-39). The context is about God's dispensational dealings with Israel and the Gentiles as groups of people. In the context he is speaking to the Gentiles at large (v.13).

What do the trees and branches represent? The olive tree is not the church. The church in this present age is a spiritual Body in which there is neither Jew nor Gentile, not a tree with Jewish and Gentile branches.

- The olive tree = Israel (Rom. 9:3-5) is likened to various trees in scripture (fig, vine, olive, bramble, see Judg. 9:7-21). The olive tree symbolizes their spiritual privileges (v.16, 28; 15:8) and access to God (Ps. 52:8).

- SOME of the branches broken off = unbelieving Israel.
- The wild olive tree = Gentiles, wild because not watched over and cared for by God.

The wild olive tree being "graffed in" represents Gentiles being brought into a position to partake of God's blessings as never before. The salvation accomplished by Israel's Messiah is now offered freely to all men. The scripture, which came through Jews, is now translated and published through the Gentiles.

The purpose of this passage is to warn the Gentiles. They must not become high-minded or boast against fallen Israel (v.25). They were cut off (God's severity) because of unbelief. Gentiles can only stand by faith (God's goodness). The grafting in of the Gentiles did not change the root so what do the Gentiles have to boast about when they are partaking of Israel's blessings? What have the Gentiles done with the goodness of God? The majority of this world rejects the word of God that has been made available to them. The Gentiles will not always have this position of direct blessings from God without Israel. They will be broken off in unbelief and Israel as a nation will be grafted back into their own tree! That's exactly what the next verses reveal.

Israel's Future Salvation

(25) For I would not, brethren, that ye should be ignorant of this mystery, lest ye should be wise in your own conceits; that blindness in part is happened to Israel, until the fulness of the Gentiles be come in.

Paul now addresses the church in particular ("brethren"). This is the first mystery (divine secret, Rom. 16:25) we come to in the order of Paul's epistles (1 Cor. 4:1), and it concerns how this present age began.

This is the second of six times that Paul says he would not have us to be ignorant of a certain thing (Rom. 1:13; 1 Cor. 10:1; 12:1; 2 Cor. 1:8; 1 Thess. 4:13). Ironically, most Christians today seem to be ignorant of the very things he mentions in those passages. The majority of professing Christians are taught the church has replaced Israel, that they are spiritual Israel, and that the covenants God made with Israel are being spiritually fulfilled in the church. Therefore, they are wise in their own conceits because they are ignorant of this mystery. They are conceited because they think that the whole Bible is all about them. Their theme song is, "Every Promise in the Book is Mine."

That the Gentiles would be given the opportunity to receive the word of God while Israel as a nation is set aside in blindness was a mystery revealed through Paul and not found in the OT scriptures. Israel being blinded was not a mystery (vv.7-10), and neither was Gentiles being blessed. Gentiles being saved through the fall and blindness of Israel was a mystery because according to prophecy, the Gentiles were to be saved through the rise of Israel.

The blindness of Israel is not complete and eternal, but rather partial (some believed) and temporary ("until"). To believe the church replaced Israel is to be ignorant of this mystery, to be wise in your own conceits (Prov. 26:12), and to attack the character of God. This chapter makes it crystal clear that God is not finished with Israel, and that He will yet save His chosen nation. Replacement Theology is the conceited wisdom of men, but Dispensational Truth is the deep wisdom of God (v.33).

The first recorded miracle of Paul illustrates how this present age began (Acts 13:1-13).

- The Jew (Bar-Jesus = son of the Savior) failed to bring God's light to the Gentile (Sergius Paulus).
- The Jew rejected word of God, but the Gentile desired to hear it.
- The Jew sought to turn the Gentile from the truth.
- The Jew was blinded, and the Gentile was saved as a result.

What is the "fulness of the Gentiles?" The common views are that it either refers to completion of the Body of Christ or the "times of the Gentiles" (Lk. 21:24). While it is true that God will resume His dealings with Israel when He catches away the Body of Christ (which implies the completion of the Body, made up primarily of believing Gentiles), and that the times of the Gentiles having the kingdoms of this world will end when Israel is saved as a nation at the second coming of Christ, neither is the context of this passage.

The word "fulness" refers to that which is complete or fulfilled. Israel's fullness concerns God fulfilling all that He promised them (v.12). The fulness of the Gentiles will come in when God is finished with His temporary arrangement in this age of giving the Gentiles an opportunity to come directly to Him without Israel.

(26) And so all Israel shall be saved: as it is written, There shall come out of Sion the Deliverer, and shall turn away ungodliness from Jacob:
(27) For this is my covenant unto them, when I shall take away their sins.

It has been prophesied (Isa. 59:20-21, and in many other passages) that the Lord will save Israel as a nation when He returns to set up His righteous kingdom on the earth and puts them under the new covenant (Acts 3:19-21; Heb. 8:8-13). That "all Israel" will be saved refers to the true believing Israel of God (from all 12 tribes), not to every Jew who has ever lived (Rom. 9:6). Israel rejected Christ in His first coming because they wanted to be saved from the Gentiles but not from their sins (Matt. 1:21).

(28) As concerning the gospel, they are enemies for your sakes: but as touching the election, they are beloved for the fathers' sakes.
(29) For the gifts and calling of God are without repentance.

That Paul referred to Israel as an enemy of God proves that the church is not Israel. Concerning the gospel ministry in this present age God counts Israel an enemy just as He does all lost sinners (Rom. 5:10) for there is now NO DIFFERENCE between Jews and Gentiles (Rom. 3:22-23). They have also been enemies of the church (1 Thess. 2:14-16). However, that does not nullify the promises that God made to their fathers (Deut. 7:6-8). God may change in how He deals with man, but the gifts and calling of God are without repentance (Num. 23:16-24; Rom. 9:4-5). The covenants that God made with Abraham (nation, land) and David (kingdom) are everlasting and will be fulfilled under the new covenant (Jer. 31:31-37).

Mercy Upon All

Study Notes

(30) For as ye in times past have not believed God, yet have now obtained mercy through their unbelief:
(31) Even so have these also now not believed, that through your mercy they also may obtain mercy.
(32) For God hath concluded them all in unbelief, that he might have mercy upon all.

Since the Gentiles, who in times past did not believe God, have obtained mercy in this present age through the fall of Israel, believing Gentiles should show mercy on unbelieving Jews by sharing the gospel with them that they might also obtain God's mercy. Also, God's mercy on the Gentiles provoked some Jews to get saved (v.11, 14).

God has concluded the whole world in unbelief that He might have mercy upon all sinners, both Jews and Gentiles, and reconcile them into one Body. That the scriptures have concluded all under sin (Gal. 3:22) proves that it is the LIVING word of God.

(33) O the depth of the riches both of the wisdom and knowledge of God! how unsearchable are his judgments, and his ways past finding out!
(34) For who hath known the mind of the Lord? or who hath been his counsellor?
(35) Or who hath first given to him, and it shall be recompensed unto him again?
(36) For of him, and through him, and to him, are all things: to whom be glory for ever. Amen.

That Paul concludes the dispensational section in worship shows that studying the Bible dispensationally should not be a cold academic pursuit. True worship is based on the truth of scripture (Jn. 4:24). There is nothing more important than knowing God and His plan and purpose for the ages. The mystery of this age is a great demonstration of God's wisdom (Eph. 3:8-11).

Nobody can know God's judgments, ways, and mind unless He reveals it (1 Cor. 2:16). The Bible is not everything God knows, but it is everything He wants us to know and that we need to know. The Calvinists love verse 36, but the "all things" in the context are the things in God's judgments and ways (v.33).

Romans 12

In the last five chapters the Holy Spirit describes what should be the character and conduct of those who are justified freely by God's grace. We are not saved by works, but we are saved unto good works (Eph. 2:8-10). The apostle Paul always laid a doctrinal foundation before making practical applications. What we truly believe determines how we behave.

In this section our conduct is dealt with in relation to:
1) The Lord (12:1-2)
2) The Church (12:3-8)
3) The Brethren (12:9-13)
4) Our Enemies (12:14-21)
5) The Higher Powers (13:1-7)
6) Society (13:8-13)
7) The Weaker Brethren (14:1-15:7)

The foundation of this whole section is the first two verses of this chapter because if we live by these verses, which reveal principles of true consecration (i.e., being separated unto God), the rest will fall into place.

True Consecration

(1) I beseech you therefore, brethren, by the mercies of God, that ye present your bodies a living sacrifice, holy, acceptable unto God, which is your reasonable service.

The "brethren" are those in the Body of Christ (v.5). Paul used the word "beseech" twenty-one times in his epistles, and this is the first reference (67 in Bible, 30 in NT). To "beseech" is to earnestly request (Phile. 8-10). That Paul used this word more than any other Bible writer is fitting since we are not under the law but grace.

The word "therefore" (v.1) tells us that this exhortation is based on what was previously said. It is based on the doctrine in the first eight chapters, but also, on what he just said and the end of the previous chapter (Rom. 11:30-36). God's amazing mercy and wisdom should motivate us to serve Him.

To present our body is to offer it willingly. We are to submissively yield our members as instruments of righteousness to God. This is an ongoing process and not a one-time event. Why did Paul say we are to present our body instead of our soul or spirit? He is dealing with our conduct and behavior. Our soul and spirit are within our body. If we present our body a living sacrifice it is evidence that we have already yielded to God inwardly (Rom. 6:6, 11-13).

To be holy is to be set apart unto God. The Bible doesn't regulate holiness to the invisible realm. The first thing that is called holy in the Bible is "GROUND" (Ex. 3:5). We have a spirit, soul, and body (1 Thess. 5:23), and we belong to God inside and out (1 Cor. 6:19-20). True holiness starts on the inside and shows up on the outside (2 Cor. 7:1).

We are to offer our body as a living sacrifice which stands in contrast to the dead sacrifices under the law. Under the law the sacrifices had to be "holy" and "acceptable" to God (Mal. 1:6-14).

Study Notes

Most of us, like Peter, would profess to be willing to die for the Lord, but He asks us to live for Him. Many professing Christians today will not sacrifice self in order to faithfully serve God (Eph. 5:1-2; Phil. 2:17).

The right standard for Christian living is not what is acceptable to us, but what is acceptable to God (Eph. 5:8-12).

In light of the great salvation God has freely given us, it is only REASONABLE that we should serve Him. Israel was to serve God in the exact way that God appointed (Rom. 9:4). Today we don't have to go to a certain building at a certain location and go through ceremonies in order to serve God. Our service is to present OURSELVES to God (2 Cor. 5:14-15; 8:5).

(2) And be not conformed to this world: but be ye transformed by the renewing of your mind, that ye may prove what is that good, and acceptable, and perfect, will of God.

There is both a negative and positive aspect to this verse and they work together like battery cables in a car.

The word "conformed" means, "Made to resemble; reduced to a likeness of; agreeable to; suited" (Webster's 1828 Dictionary). Satan and his world system seeks to conform us from the outside in (Gen. 3:6).

Bible-believers have a negative view of the world. We know that it is an EVIL world (Gal. 1:4) because:
   1) Its "god" (Satan) is evil (2 Cor. 4:4)
   2) Its people are evil (Jn. 15:18; Eph. 2:2)

3) Its ways are evil (Eph. 2:3, 1 John 2:15-17)

We are to not to think or act like this present evil world (Eph. 4:17-24). Biblical separation is not isolation but contact without contamination. The popular philosophy of churches today is that we must be like the world to reach the world. Christ was a friend of sinners, but He was still separate from them (Heb. 7:26). A ship in the water is appropriate but water in the ship can be disastrous!

If we are not being transformed, we are being conformed. There is no neutral ground in spiritual warfare. Neither in world-conformity nor Christian transformation are we the agents to bring it to pass: the verbs are passive in both cases.

To be transformed is to be completely changed from the inside out. How does this change come? By the renewing of the MIND (2 Cor. 3:18; 4:16; Eph. 4:23; Col. 3:10). That is why we emphasize the importance of sound DOCTRINE. We cannot believe and live by what you don't KNOW. The battlefield in spiritual warfare is the MIND (2 Cor. 10:3-5; 11:3). God will give us a sound mind (2 Tim. 1:7) as we believe and meditate upon the sound words of scripture (2 Tim. 1:13) which teach sound doctrine (2 Tim. 4:3). Evidence of a renewed mind is to have NO confidence in flesh (v.3; Phil. 3:3).

In presenting our body and renewing our mind we will be able to know and do the will of God. The will of God is revealed the word of God (Eph. 5:17; Col. 1:9). Once we understand the big picture of what God is doing in this present age, we can make decisions about the details of life that are in line with the revealed will of God. Sadly, most people superstitiously try to discern God's will without exercising their mind in God's word.

The will of God is:
1) Good – It's good even if it's difficult (Matt. 26:38-39)
2) Acceptable – God is pleased (Eph. 1:6; 2 Cor. 5:9)
3) Perfect – How could it be anything else?

Think Soberly

(3) For I say, through the grace given unto me, to every man that is among you, not to think of himself more highly than he ought to think; but to think soberly, according as God hath dealt to every man the measure of faith.

Concerning our relationship to one another in the church Paul gives an:
- Exhortation (v.3) – Do not think more highly of yourself than you ought to think.
- Explanation (vv.4-5) – We are members of one another.
- Application (vv.6-8) – We have different gifts to serve one another.

The apostle Paul emphasized, by inspiration, that the Lord gave him the grace to be a faithful minister to the Gentiles and the Body of Christ (Rom. 15:15-16; 1 Cor. 3:10; Gal. 2:9; Eph. 3:1-12). His exhortation to humility is powerful because he practiced what he preached. He magnified his office (Rom. 11:13), but not himself (1 Cor. 15:9-10; Eph. 3:8).

To think highly of our self is to be lifted up in pride. What do we have to be proud of (Rom. 7:18)? Any good thing in us or about us is because of Jesus Christ (Phile. 6). We do not need high self-esteem or low self-esteem. We are to esteem Christ, who is our identity, and His word (Job 23:12). We are complete in Christ and accepted in the beloved. We are to think soberly (i.e., seriously) and in accordance with what God has made us to be in Christ (2 Cor. 5:16-17). This comes by the renewing of our mind (v.2). We are also not to think too highly of ministers (1 Cor. 4:6-7).

In relation to other believers, we are to think with the same mind toward them as members of one Body (v.16; Eph. 4:1-2; Phil. 2:1-5). One member is not better than another. Every member is important in the Body of Christ (Eph. 4:7, 16). God has given EVERY member a function in the Body and the measure of grace and faith needed to fulfill it (2 Cor. 10:12-18).

One Body in Christ

(4) For as we have many members in one body, and all members have not the same office:
(5) So we, being many, are one body in Christ, and every one members one of another.

Paul used the human body to illustrate the spiritual Body of Christ. God has given every member of the Body a function and purpose (1 Cor. 12:12-27).

Although Paul had not yet been to Rome when he wrote this epistle, he was in the same Body with the believers in Rome. I have known Baptists who deny the truth of an invisible and spiritual church. They claim a church can only be local and visible, and that every scriptural church is a Body of Christ. If that were true, the church could not assemble on earth because our Head is in Heaven! We are called out of the world and assembled by one Spirit in Christ (Eph. 2:6).

There are many local churches (Rom. 16:3-5, 16) but there is only ONE BODY (1 Cor. 10:17; 12:12-13; Eph. 2:16; 4:4-6; Col. 3:15). The local assembly is to be a visible manifestation of the spiritual Body in a community (1 Tim. 3:14-16).

(6) Having then gifts differing according to the grace that is given to us, whether prophecy, let us prophesy according to the proportion of faith;
(7) Or ministry, let us wait on our ministering: or he that teacheth, on teaching;
(8) Or he that exhorteth, on exhortation: he that giveth, let him do it with simplicity; he that ruleth, with diligence; he that sheweth mercy, with cheerfulness.

This is one of three passages in Paul's epistles on the gifts of the Spirit. The Holy Spirit gives believers the desire and ability to do things in the ministry that are beyond our natural ability. Each passage has a different emphasis.

1) In Romans 12:6-8 the emphasis is on the ministry gifts.
2) In 1 Corinthians 12-14 the emphasis is on miraculous sign gifts (1 Cor. 12:4-11). The church at Corinth was a carnal church full of problems and yet Paul said they came behind in no gift (1 Cor. 1:7). That proves the sign gifts were not reserved for the super spiritual saints. They were supernatural manifestations that the Holy Ghost

gave during the transition period. They were to be used for the edification of believers and signs to the unbelieving Jews (1 Cor. 14:20-22).

3) In Ephesians 4:7-16 the emphasis is on the men God uses (Acts 20:28). The foundational gifts of apostles and prophets are no longer needed, but evangelists (taking the gospel where it is not being preached) and pastors (leading and feeding God's people) certainly are. All believers are to "do the work of an evangelist" (2 Tim. 4:5), but not all are evangelists. That believers are to teach others what they have learned does not mean all have the gift of teaching.

There are three main views concerning spiritual gifts.
1) All are still in operation today.
2) None are in operation today.
3) Some are in operation today.

God used some of the gifts for divine revelation and signs (e.g., prophecy, miracles, healing, and tongues). Those ceased with the completion of the transition period away from Israel and the completion of the word of God (1 Cor. 13:8-13). The miraculous signs gifts are no longer needed (1 Cor. 12:7; 14:4; 2 Tim. 3:16).

There are gifts that still have a purpose today (6 of the 7 in Rom. 12) and nowhere does Paul teach that all ministry gifts will cease. Some of my right division brethren seem to believe that God is not doing anything supernatural today. Yet, the scripture, salvation, and the Christian life are supernatural!

God gives each member of the Body the measure of faith and grace needed to use their gift in the work of the ministry (v.3b).

We have a responsibility to stir up the gift (2 Tim. 1:6) and not to neglect it (1 Tim. 4:14).

1) Prophecy – Speaking divine revelation by the Spirit ("proportion" = "in part").
2) Ministry – Faithfully serving to meet the needs of others (deacons).
3) Teaching – Teaching the scripture (doctrine).
4) Exhortation – Preaching the scripture (application).
5) Giving – The ability and desire to go above and beyond in giving to the cause of Christ. Giving with simplicity has to do with the right motive.
6) Ruling – The local church is to be ruled by elders (1 Tim. 5:17).
7) Mercy – Cheerfully seeking to work with those that are overlooked and restore those overtaken in a fault (Gal. 6:1).

While we may not have all these gifts, we should all serve, give, and show mercy.

Practical Admonitions

This is one of the most practical passages in the Bible concerning the Christian walk. It describes how we should live as a result of being transformed by the renewing of our mind (v.2). There are twenty-five admonitions given in verses 9-21.

(9) Let love be without dissimulation. Abhor that which is evil; cleave to that which is good.

The first admonition is foundational to the rest. The word "dissimulation" is only used one other time in the Bible and that passage helps us understand what the word means (hypocrisy, Gal. 2:11-14). In the word dissimulation we see the word simulation which means imitation or counterfeit (2 Cor. 6:6; 1 Pet. 1:22).

When we are newly saved our love for God and others is real. However, because we still have the flesh our love can grow cold if we yield to the flesh instead of the Spirit. Those that have been saved for a while can fall into the trap of going through the motions of the Christian life without the sincere motivation of real love. We know how to act like we love God and others but is too often with dissimulation.

Real love will result in obedience to all the other admonitions that follow. We must not just talk about how we love others; we must walk in it (Eph. 5:1-2; 1 Jn. 3:16-18). Love is the fulfilling of the moral law (Rom. 13:8-10).

According to the Oxford English Dictionary, to "abhor" something is to regard it with "horror, extreme repugnance or disgust, to hate utterly, loathe, abominate."

It is not loving to accept anything and everything. That God is love (1 Jn. 4:8, 16) does not cancel out His hatred for certain things (Prov. 6:16; 1 Jn. 1:5). If we truly love God, we will hate evil (Ps. 97:10; 119:128). This present world system is EVIL (Gal. 1:4). Our love for God will cause us to be separated from the world and religion unto God. We will separate from what we hate. By the way, if we are not careful, our separation can be with dissimulation if it is motivated by self-righteousness.

The word "cleave" can either mean to divide or unite depending on the context of usage. These opposite definitions go together because in order to cling to something you must of necessity depart from other things (Gen. 2:24). A man who loves his wife will be separated from all other women. We are to cleave to the Lord (Acts 11:23). If we do, we will separate from all that is contrary to Him. We will abhor what He calls evil and cleave to what He says is good.

(10) Be kindly affected one to another with brotherly love; in honour preferring one another;

This one verse, if practiced, would prevent most church cliques and splits. All believers love the brethren (1 Thess. 4:9-10). However, we often fail to SHOW it by being kindly affectioned one to another. The word "affectioned" has to do with the feelings of our heart. It will show up in kind words and deeds (Eph. 4:30-32). We will prefer that others are honored before us. Servants have no problem letting others be first (Phil. 2:3-5).

(11) Not slothful in business; fervent in spirit; serving the Lord;

The word "business," as used in this verse, refers to "serious engagement; important occupation; in distinction from trivial affairs" (Webster's 1828 Dictionary). Serving the Lord is the most important business in the world! We are dealing in ETERNAL matters. Everything else is trivial in comparison. If we really believe that we will be fervent (i.e., on fire, 2 Pet. 3:12) in spirit as we serve the Lord. Laziness is still a sin.

Sadly, secular businessmen usually demonstrate more fervency in conducting their business than we do in the church. If someone paid you a thousand dollars for every soul that you witnessed to for Christ, would you witness to more people?

Being fervent will make us diligent (Prov. 22:29; Acts 18:25). Evangelizing the sinners and edifying the saints should be a labor of love.

We should serve the Lord with our spirit (Rom. 1:9). If we have a burning desire on the inside to serve the Lord, we will not require outside motivation. Everything we do for the Lord is important business. We serve the Lord by serving others (Rom. 12:1-8). We should have fervent charity (1 Pet. 4:8) and pray fervently for one another (Col. 4:12-13).

(12) Rejoicing in hope; patient in tribulation; continuing instant in prayer;

The Body of Christ will not go through the prophesied tribulation period, which is the "time of Jacob's trouble" (Jer. 30:7), but we will face tribulation in this present evil world (1 Thess. 3:1-4). How can we patiently endure tribulation? Patience is "the suffering of afflictions, pain, toil, calamity, provocation, or other evils with a calm unruffled temper; endurance without murmuring or fretfulness" (Webster's 1828 Dictionary). Rejoicing in our blessed hope and continuing instant in prayer will enable us to be patient in tribulation (Rom. 5:1-5; 8:25-28).

We should be always rejoicing (Phil. 4:4) and praying (Eph. 6:18). Continuing instant in prayer means we are always ready to pray (e.g., Neh. 2:4-5).

(13) Distributing to the necessity of saints; given to hospitality.

All believers are "saints" because we are sanctified in Christ. This distribution is not the same as we find in the early Acts period (Acts 4:31-35). We must trust God to provide for us as we work to take care of our own family (1 Thess. 4:11-12; 2 Thess. 3:10-12). However, any of us can fall on hard times. A church family should willingly distribute of their abundance to provide for the needs of its members (1 Tim. 6:17-18). This is not limited to our own local church (Rom. 15:25-26). Giving to the poor is a Bible principle. The priority in giving should be the household of faith (Gal. 6:6, 10).

Hospitality is "the act or practice of receiving and entertaining strangers or guests without reward, or with kind and generous liberality" (Webster's 1828 Dictionary). A bishop must be "given to hospitality" (1 Tim. 3:2). Since the bishop is to be an example, all believers should also be given to hospitality. It must be willingly and sincere (1 Pet. 4:9). The early churches met in houses because that was the only place they could meet. Having guests in your house was a much more common occurrence in those days than it is for us. Wherever we meet, the local church should be a warm and welcoming place to be.

(14) Bless them which persecute you: bless, and curse not.

Paul takes it for granted that believers will suffer persecution (2 Tim. 3:12). This is not an easy command to obey (Acts 23:1-3). Paul was not sinless, but he was a good example in practicing what he preached (1 Cor. 4:11-17). Although the unbelieving Jews persecuted him, he was burdened for them and desired to see them saved (Rom. 9:1-3; 10:1). Jesus Christ is the only one who perfectly obeyed it (Lk. 23:34), we can only do it through His power. Stephen was able to do it because he was filled with the Holy Ghost (Acts 7:60).

There is a difference between moral truth and dispensational truth. This is the same moral principle that Christ taught in the constitution of His kingdom (Matt. 5:43-48). However, there are some doctrinal differences between the sermon on the mount and Paul's epistles (cf. Matt. 6:14-15; Eph. 4:32). The carnal mind bristles at this principle because it fears being taken advantage of. If we bless those who persecute us, such a response may lead them to repentance (Prov. 15:1; Rom. 12:21). If not, vengeance belongs to God (v.19).

(15) Rejoice with them that do rejoice, and weep with them that weep.

Jesus didn't weep at the wedding in Cana of Galilee or rejoice at the tomb of Lazarus (Ecc. 3:1, 4). If we love others, we will be mindful of their situation and act accordingly. Don't be envious when others have cause for rejoicing; rejoice with them. Don't take the weeping of others lightly; weep with them. Let's not be like Job's "friends" who were "miserable comforters." It is better to weep with those that weep than it is to lecture them or tell them about your problems.

(16) Be of the same mind one toward another. Mind not high things, but condescend to men of low estate. Be not wise in your own conceits.

The apostle Paul exhorted believers to be of the "same mind" three times (1 Cor. 1:11; Phil. 4:2) and of "one mind" four times (Rom. 15:6; 2 Cor. 13:11; Phil. 1:27; 2:2). This does not mean we agree on every little thing, but that we think with the mind of Christ (1 Cor. 2:16; Phil. 2:5) according to the fundamental truths of scripture. We are to see one another as members of the same Body.

We are not to set our mind on being above others (Rom. 12:3). We may have a position that is above others, but we are to use that position and authority to serve (Prov. 16:18-19; Matt. 23:5-12). To "condescend" is to descend or come down voluntarily (Ps. 136:1, 23; Matt. 11:28-30; Lk. 1:46-48; 1 Tim. 6:17-18). A Christian master should have fellowship with his Christian servants (e.g., Phile. 15-17). We are not to show partiality in the church (Jam. 2:1-4).

Conceit refers to that which is conceived in the mind. We must look to God's word for wisdom (Prov. 3:5-7). There is a wisdom that is earthly, sensual, and devilish (Jam. 3:13-18). Those that fail to rightly divide the word of truth are not thinking with the wisdom of God but are wise in their own conceit (Rom. 11:25).

(17) Recompense to no man evil for evil. Provide things honest in the sight of all men.

To recompense is to pay back (Prov. 24:28-29; 1 Thess. 5:15; 1 Pet. 3:9). Instead of paying back evil for evil, we are to recompense good.

We are to walk honestly before God and all men in all matters (2 Cor. 1:12; 4:1-2; 8:21; 1 Thess. 5:11-12).

(18) If it be possible, as much as lieth in you, live peaceably with all men.
We are to be peacemakers, not troublemakers. If someone has strife with us it should be their fault and not our own. If the peace of God rules our hearts, we should be at peace among one another (Col. 3:12-15).

Sometimes it is not possible to live peaceably with all men. We are not to be pacifists to the point of allowing someone to hurt our family. Christians may defend themselves and their loved ones. When Christ taught His disciples to "resist not evil" (Matt. 5:38-40), it was not the same dispensational context in which we are living. We live in a "present evil world" and the kingdom of heaven is not at hand.

(19) Dearly beloved, avenge not yourselves, but rather give place unto wrath: for it is written, Vengeance is mine; I will repay, saith the Lord.

We are not to take matters in our own hands and usurp God's authority (Deut. 32:35). We must give wrath over to God and not allow it to fill our hearts (Eph. 4:30-32).

(20) Therefore if thine enemy hunger, feed him; if he thirst, give him drink: for in so doing thou shalt heap coals of fire on his head.
(21) Be not overcome of evil, but overcome evil with good.

We are more likely to overcome evil by doing good to our enemies than by seeking revenge (Prov. 25:21-22). It will bring them conviction, and if they persist in evil, it will bring them greater judgment (Rom. 2:4-5). Remember what Christ did for us when we were His enemies (Rom. 5:8-10).

The only way to faithfully walk in accordance with all these admonitions is to walk in the Spirit. Christ lived by these, and He will live through us (Gal. 2:20).

Romans 13

This chapter concerns our relationship toward human government. Christians should be the best citizens in their country. God did not call the church to overthrow government; we have more important work to do as ambassadors for Christ (2 Cor. 5:20).

Paul gives four good reasons for being subject to human government.

I. For Wrath's Sake (vv.1-4)
II. For Conscience's Sake (vv.5-7)
III. For Love's Sake (vv.8-10)
IV. For Our Saviour's Sake (vv.11-14)

For Wrath's Sake

(1) Let every soul be subject unto the higher powers. For there is no power but of God: the powers that be are ordained of God.
(2) Whosoever therefore resisteth the power, resisteth the ordinance of God: and they that resist shall receive to themselves damnation.
(3) For rulers are not a terror to good works, but to the evil. Wilt thou then not be afraid of the power? do that which is good, and thou shalt have praise of the same:
(4) For he is the minister of God to thee for good. But if thou do that which is evil, be afraid; for he beareth not

the sword in vain: for he is the minister of God, a revenger to execute wrath upon him that doeth evil.

This instruction is not just for the saved, but for "every soul." The "higher powers" refer to governmental authorities. We are to be subject to them whether they are saved or not (Titus 3:1-3). Not only are we not to speak evil AGAINST them, but we are to make intercession FOR them (1 Tim. 2:1-4).

We must acknowledge that government officials are ministers of God. This passage does not teach that God puts every official in office but simply that He ordained human government (Gen. 9:6). To disobey authority that God has ordained is to disobey God (v.2). The root reason there is such a lack of respect for authority in our country is that most people do not fear God.

The basic function of government is to protect the good and punish the evil (1 Pet. 2:13-17). The "damnation" (v.2) Paul warns us about is "the sword" (v.4) of capital punishment (Gen. 9:5-6; Acts 25:11). Those who live a good Christian life typically do not have to worry about the government punishing them. However, when a government calls good evil and evil good (Isa. 5:20), there will be problems.

When the government punishes those who are good, they are no longer ministers of God for good, and we are not obligated to submit to their abuse of power (e.g., 2 Cor. 11:32-33). If the government tells us to disobey God, then we are to disobey the government and trust God with the consequences. The Bible does not teach that we are to unconditionally obey the government (Ex. 1:15-21; Dan. 3, 6; Acts 4:18-20; 5:27-29, 40-42).

The THIRTEEN (the number associated with separation) original colonies knew something about Romans 13! In America, we have been given great liberty that has been secured by a great price. When authorities abuse their power and go against their own laws, we have the freedom to resist and protest. The apostle Paul used his rights as a Roman citizen (Acts 22:25-29; 25:10-11).

For Conscience's Sake

(5) Wherefore ye must needs be subject, not only for wrath, but also for conscience sake.
(6) For for this cause pay ye tribute also: for they are God's ministers, attending continually upon this very thing.
(7) Render therefore to all their dues: tribute to whom tribute is due; custom to whom custom; fear to whom fear; honour to whom honour.

Paul had much to say about the conscience (21x's in his epistles). Webster's 1828 Dictionary defines it as, "Internal or self-knowledge, or judgment of right and wrong; or the faculty, power or principle within us, which decides on the lawfulness or unlawfulness of our own actions and affections, and instantly approves or condemns them."

We know in our conscience that it is right to submit to God-ordained authority. Of course, it is possible the conscience to be weak (1 Cor. 8:12), defiled (Titus 1:15), or even seared (1 Tim. 4:2).

It costs money to operate the government. Sadly, the greediness of human nature leads many government officials to raise taxes beyond what is necessary.

It is right for us to render what is due:
1) Tribute – tax on a person, house, or land (Matt. 17:24-27; 22:15-22)
2) Custom – tax on merchandise
3) Respect – fear and honor

For Love's Sake

(8) Owe no man any thing, but to love one another: for he that loveth another hath fulfilled the law.
(9) For this, Thou shalt not commit adultery, Thou shalt not kill, Thou shalt not steal, Thou shalt not bear false witness, Thou shalt not covet; and if there be any other commandment, it is briefly comprehended in this saying, namely, Thou shalt love thy neighbour as thyself.
(10) Love worketh no ill to his neighbour: therefore love is the fulfilling of the law.

It is not wise to take on monetary debt that cannot be repaid in a timely manner (Prov. 22:7). There are spiritual debts we always owe as Christians (Rom. 1:14-16; Rom. 8:12).

While believers live under the law of the land, we also live under a much higher law as a citizen of heaven: the law of love (Gal. 6:2). We are to love "all men" (1 Thess. 3:12). If we love God and our neighbor, we will fulfill the righteousness of the law (Matt. 22:35-40). Loving God will motivate us to keep the first five commandments, loving our neighbor the last five.

We are not under the law of Moses and if we are led of the Spirit there is no need to be (Gal. 5:13-16). The apostle Paul applied nine of the ten commandments to the Body of Christ under grace. We are not under the sabbath (Col. 2:16) which was given as a sign between God and Israel (Ex. 31:13).

The NIV and other modern versions omit "thou shalt not bear false witness" from verse 9. This exact list of the last five commandants exposes how the Roman Catholic Church makes the tenth commandment two separate commandments (thou shalt not covet they neighbor's wife and thy neighbor's goods) in order to omit the second commandment (no graven images) which they constantly break.

For Our Saviour's Sake

We have now reached the pinnacle of motives in this passage: from fear to conscience to love for others to devotion to Christ.

Two of the greatest motivations for living right is love (vv.8-10) and knowing that the coming of the Lord is near (vv.11-14).

In the context the apostle Paul is applying the doctrine set forth in the first main section of this epistle to our conduct. Paul's epistles present a perfect balance of doctrine and practice. This short passage is an example of that balance. What we KNOW (v.11) should make a difference in how we WALK (vv.12-14).

(11) And that, knowing the time, that now it is high time to awake out of sleep: for now is our salvation nearer than when we believed.
(12) The night is far spent, the day is at hand: ...

Study Notes

Why is Paul writing to believers about a future salvation? In the first part of this epistle, we learned about the three tenses of salvation.

1) Past: Justification – We were saved from the penalty of sin (Rom. 5:1).
2) Present: Sanctification – We are being saved from the power of sin in our daily walk (Rom. 6:14).
3) Future: Glorification – We will be saved from the presence of sin (Rom. 8:23-25) when the Lord comes.

The salvation Paul is referring to here is the rapture (Rom. 5:9-10). When Christ catches us off the earth, we will be saved from the wrath to come (1 Thess. 1:10; 5:9; 2 Thess. 2:13-14), and our bodies will be redeemed (Eph. 1:13-14; 4:30; Phil. 3:20-21).

The expression "high time" originated with the use of the hourglass. When the sand in an hourglass is high it means that time is almost up (1 Cor. 7:29). There are many expressions in the English-speaking world that originated with the KJB. Paul is saying that it is time for believers to wake up to the reality of the imminent coming of Christ for the church. It could happen any moment! We should never be asleep to this truth because we are to be LOOKING for the blessed hope (Titus 2:13). There are no signs that must precede it as with the second coming. We are not in the "times and seasons" of prophecy (1 Thess. 5:1). We are to be looking for Christ from heaven and not the antichrist from earth. Each day that passes means that it is nearer than it ever was before. God never said how long this mystery age of His longsuffering would last (2 Cor. 6:2). What we know about the time of the rapture is that it is nearer than it was yesterday.

Therefore, we should be redeeming the time and not wasting it (Eph. 5:16; Col. 4:5).

- **"the night is far spent"** – This present evil world is in spiritual darkness (Gal. 1:4; Eph. 6:12; Phil. 2:15; Col. 1:13).

- **"the day is at hand"** – The day Paul is talking about is the day of the rapture and judgement seat of Christ (Phil. 1:10; 2:16). That "the day" is "at hand" (i.e., near, Matt. 26:46-47) means it is imminent (Phil. 3:20; 4:5). This proves that the "day of Christ" in 2 Thess. 2:2 is not referring to the blessed hope of our rapture, but to the second coming of Christ in judgment which Paul said is NOT "at hand." The "day of Christ," like the "day of the Lord," does not refer to just one event, the context determines what it is referring to.

Paul exhorts believers to "AWAKE" three times in his epistles.

1) To the nearness of our salvation (Rom. 13:11)
2) To righteousness (1 Cor. 15:33-34)
3) To walking in the light (Eph. 5:14-17)

(12) ... let us therefore cast off the works of darkness, and let us put on the armour of light.
(13) Let us walk honestly, as in the day; not in rioting and drunkenness, not in chambering and wantonness, not in strife and envying.
(14) But put ye on the Lord Jesus Christ, and make not provision for the flesh, to fulfil the lusts thereof.

If we really believe the doctrine of the imminent and pre-tribulation rapture (we will be caught up to heaven before the seventieth week of Daniel) it will affect our daily walk. Do you truly believe that at any moment you could be caught up to meet the Lord in the air and give an account to Him at the judgment seat of Christ (Rom. 14:10)?

The right response to this doctrine is to:
1) Love the appearing of Christ (2 Tim. 4:8-10)
2) Look for Him daily (Titus 2:13)
3) Live in light of His coming (Titus 2:11-15)

Since our salvation is near, let us THEREFORE:

- **"cast off the works of darkness"** – There are six works (three pairs) mentioned in the context. Paul lists specific sins in several passages (e.g., Gal. 5:19-21). By the Spirit of God and His word, we have the power to "cast off the works of darkness."

- **"put on the armour of light"** – By comparing verse 12 with verse 14 we learn that Christ is the armour of light (v.14; 2 Cor. 6:7; 1 Thess. 5:8; Eph. 6:10-18). We put on Christ in salvation (Col. 3:9-10) but we must by faith put off the deeds of the old man and put on the new man (Eph. 4:17-32).

- **"walk honestly"** – As to our standing in Christ, we are in the light. As to our state we need to walk in the light (Eph. 5:1-13; 1 Thess. 5:1-11). To make provision for the flesh is to feed it with the things of this world. Instead of doing that we need to feed the new man with the word of God (Rom. 12:2; 1 Tim. 4:6).

Biblical separation is UNTO the Lord and FROM the world, the flesh, and the devil.

Romans 14

This chapter, and the beginning of the next (Rom. 15:1-7), is about our conduct in relation to those who are weak in the faith (Rom. 14:1; 15:1). Paul deals with the problem of questionable things and what do when sincere brethren disagree about personal practices. He recognizes that in a local church there are both strong and weak believers and it is inevitable that they will disagree on certain issues. He primarily addresses the strong because they should take the lead in resolving such disputations.

All believers have the same perfect standing in Christ (Col. 2:10) but not all believers are at the same place in their spiritual growth (Phil. 3:15-16). To be "weak in the faith" (note that he said, "THE faith," and not "in faith") is to be lacking in the spiritual knowledge and understanding of doctrinal truth. Those who are strong in the faith know and live by the meat of the word (1 Cor. 3:1-3; Heb. 5:12-14).

We must keep in mind the historical setting of this passage. It was written during the transition period in which God was using Paul's ministry to get a remnant saved by grace out of Israel into the Body of Christ before He officially set the nation aside in judicial blindness (see Rom. 11). Some of the Jewish believers were clinging to the religious customs they were raised in, while some of the Gentile believers were abusing their Christian liberty and thereby offending their Jewish brethren (see 1 Cor. 8-10). Paul had a different response toward those who were trusting in the works of the law for justification and/or sanctification (Gal.

4:10-11). Being weak in the faith is not the same as opposing the faith and causing divisions. We are not to receive such people, but rather we are to mark and avoid them (Rom. 16:17-18).

We must understand the basis of fellowship (Eph. 4:1-6) and receive all whom God receives (Rom. 14:1; 15:7). Sadly, many Christians have more requirements than God does concerning fellowship.

While the question of eating meats offered to idols is not an issue today, we still deal with similar issues. This passage contains principles by which those who are strong in the faith may know how to properly handle the differences that arise between them and those who are weak in the faith on questions of conscience and personal practice. We will consider these principles in the form of questions.

1) Am I fully persuaded? (14:1-5)
2) Am I doing this unto the Lord? (14:6-12)
3) Am I causing others to stumble? (14:13-21)
4) Am I doing this by faith? (14:22-23)
5) Am I pleasing myself or others? (15:1-7)

Am I Fully Persuaded?

(1) Him that is weak in the faith receive ye, but not to doubtful disputations.
(2) For one believeth that he may eat all things: another, who is weak, eateth herbs.
(3) Let not him that eateth despise him that eateth not; and let not him which eateth not judge him that eateth: for God hath received him.

(4) Who art thou that judgest another man's servant? to his own master he standeth or falleth. Yea, he shall be holden up: for God is able to make him stand.

(5) One man esteemeth one day above another: another esteemeth every day alike. Let every man be fully persuaded in his own mind.

Every believer has personal soul liberty before the Lord (2 Cor. 1:24). Since we are not under the law but under grace, when it comes to things not clearly and expressly laid out in scripture, we have the liberty to be fully persuaded (or, convinced) in our own mind. We are not to be convinced by tradition, experience, popularity, or feelings. We should seek to be fully persuaded by the Lord and His word (v.14).

We are to receive one another in sincere fellowship, not so we can dispute with one another over doubtful things (Phil. 2:14). Of course, there are things that it is right to dispute over (Acts 15:1-2; 17:16-17). Sadly, many dispute over little things and will not take a stand on major things. Like the Pharisees, they strain at a gnat and swallow a camel (Matt. 23:24).

The weak brother was so afraid of being defiled that he practically held to a vegetable diet rather than possibly partake of meat that has been offered to idols or is unclean according to Jewish law. Under grace we are permitted to eat anything (1 Tim. 4:4-5). This is a great example of dispensational truth. God does not change in His person or moral principles, but He has changed in His dealings with man through the ages.

1) Adam (Gen. 1:29) – no meat
2) Noah (Gen. 9:3-4) – meat, but without blood

3) Noah ((Lev. 11:46-47) – only "clean" meats
4) Paul (1 Tim. 4:1-5) – nothing to be refused

God receives us on the basis of Jesus Christ, not our diet or what day of the week we go to church. The one who knows that he has liberty to eat what he wants should not despise his weaker brother that lacks that knowledge. Neither should the weaker brother sit in judgment on those who understand, appreciate, and walk in the liberty we have in Christ. The weaker brethren are typically more judgmental in the wrong sense of the word.

Christians are not to judge one another in such matters. The spiritual man judges all things (1 Cor. 2:16; Phil. 1:9) but he is not hypocritical in judgment (Matt. 7:1-5) and he knows better than to sit in judgment on another person concerning questionable things. We don't have the authority (we are God's servants) or ability (we don't even know our own heart) to judge our brethren. God seeks to help us stand but sadly His people are too often trying to tear each other down.

The strong believer knows that in this present age every day is alike and that he should live every day unto the Lord. There are no holy days under grace (Col. 2:16). It is the weaker brother who thinks that Christmas, Easter, or even Sunday is more holy than any other day. The Bible never refers to Sunday as the Sabbath or the Lord's day.

Am I Doing This Unto the Lord?

(6) He that regardeth the day, regardeth it unto the Lord; and he that regardeth not the day, to the Lord he doth not regard it. He that eateth, eateth to the Lord, for he giveth

God thanks; and he that eateth not, to the Lord he eateth not, and giveth God thanks.
(7) For none of us liveth to himself, and no man dieth to himself.
(8) For whether we live, we live unto the Lord; and whether we die, we die unto the Lord: whether we live therefore, or die, we are the Lord's.
(9) For to this end Christ both died, and rose, and revived, that he might be Lord both of the dead and living.

There is nothing wrong with resting one day a week or abstaining from pork as long as we don't believe that is what makes us right with God (1 Cor. 8:8).

"I'm living my own life!" is a statement that no Christian should ever make because we belong to the Lord (Acts 20:28; 1 Cor. 6:19-20). Therefore, we must live to please Him (1 Cor. 10:31; Rom. 12:1; 2 Cor. 5:14-15; Col. 3:17, 23). There are many who want Jesus as a Saviour from hell but not as the Lord of their life, but He died and rose again to be our LORD (Phil. 2:9-13). He is worthy of our faith and obedience (Lk. 6:46; Acts 9:6), not for salvation but because of salvation (Eph. 2:8-10).

(10) But why dost thou judge thy brother? or why dost thou set at nought thy brother? for we shall all stand before the judgment seat of Christ.
(11) For it is written, As I live, saith the Lord, every knee shall bow to me, and every tongue shall confess to God.
(12) So then every one of us shall give account of himself to God.

When the Lord comes, we must all personally give an account (1 Cor. 3:10-15) for how we served Him (not for our sins which were already judged on the cross). It is the Lord alone that has the authority and ability to judge us (1 Cor. 4:1-5). The judgment seat of Christ is a great motivator for faithful Christian service (2 Cor. 5:9-10).

The corrupt modern versions (e.g., NASB, NIV, ESV) change verse 10 to say, "judgment seat of God" which weakens the passage on the deity of Christ ("judgment seat of Christ" = "give account of himself to God") and confuses people concerning the different judgments.

That every knew will bow and every tongue confess to God, as spoken by Isaiah (45:23), will be fulfilled at different judgments (see notes in Romans 2). Isaiah did not prophesy of the judgment seat of Christ; Paul applied the principle of what he said to the Body of Christ.

Am I Causing Others to Stumble?

(13) Let us not therefore judge one another any more: but judge this rather, that no man put a stumblingblock or an occasion to fall in his brother's way.

The spiritual man does not judge his brother but rather judges his own actions to be sure that he is not a stumblingblock to others (1 Cor. 2:16). This verse defines "stumblingblock" as "an occasion to fall." We cannot fall out of salvation, but we can fall into deception, temptation, and temporal condemnation. Keep in mind that the context is about legitimate issues of the conscience, not petty preferences.

(14) I know, and am persuaded by the Lord Jesus, that there is nothing unclean of itself: but to him that esteemeth any thing to be unclean, to him it is unclean.
(15) But if thy brother be grieved with thy meat, now walkest thou not charitably. Destroy not him with thy meat, for whom Christ died.

The believer that is strong in the faith knows that what he eats cannot make him unclean in and of itself, whether it be pork or meat that had been used in idolatrous sacrifice (Matt. 15:17-20; Acts 10:9-16). The same God who pronounced certain meats unclean for Israel has pronounced all meats clean for the Body of Christ (1 Tim. 4:4-5). However, charity will cause him to not eat such things in front of a weaker brother that lacks that knowledge (1 Cor. 8:13).

The word "destroy" (v.15) concerns the spiritual STATE of a believer (the work of God, v.20; Eph. 2:10; Phil. 1:6), not their STANDING. The weaker brother is "damned" (v.23) in a temporal sense if he eats with a doubtful conscience.

(16) Let not then your good be evil spoken of:

It is possible to do a right thing in a wrong manner that causes others to stumble and speak evil of what we did.

(17) For the kingdom of God is not meat and drink; but righteousness, and peace, and joy in the Holy Ghost.
(18) For he that in these things serveth Christ is acceptable to God, and approved of men.

Some use verse 17 to teach that the "kingdom of God" never refers to a literal and visible kingdom. The kingdom of God is not limited to Israel's program (69x's in NT; 8x's in Paul's epistles). It is broader in scope than the kingdom of heaven. When the kingdom of heaven (32x's in Matthew) is established on the earth at the second coming of Christ, the spiritual and eternal kingdom of God will be manifest on the earth. The kingdom of heaven was postponed at the fall of Israel, but we spiritually enter the kingdom of God upon salvation (Col. 1:13). We will inherit the kingdom of God upon the rapture (1 Cor. 15:50-52) to reign with Him in His heavenly kingdom (2 Tim. 4:18). The judgment seat of Christ will determine the reward of our inheritance (Col. 3:22-25).

(19) Let us therefore follow after the things which make for peace, and things wherewith one may edify another.

To "follow after" something is to pursue it. We should not be pursuing our own rights and privileges but living peaceably with the brethren and the things that edify them (1 Pet. 3:8-11). We are to pursue peace, but never by compromising the truth (Rom. 12:18; Jam. 3:17).

We are also to follow after:
1) Charity (1 Cor. 14:1)
2) Christ and being conformed to His image (Phil. 3:12-16)
3) Spiritual qualities (1 Tim. 6:11)

(20) For meat destroy not the work of God. All things indeed are pure; but it is evil for that man who eateth with offence.

(21) It is good neither to eat flesh, nor to drink wine, nor any thing whereby thy brother stumbleth, or is offended, or is made weak.

Am I Doing this by Faith?

To destroy (i.e., tear down) the work of God is the opposite of edification (i.e., build up). In the context, the "all things" that are pure refers to meats (v.14; Titus 1:15). Under grace we have the liberty to eat whatever we want, but it is evil to abuse our liberty and cause our brother to stumble, be offended, or made weak (1 Cor. 8-10 should be studied along with this passage). Christian liberty is not about our personal rights but serving one another (Gal. 5:13).

Drinking wine was part of the idolatrous worship in pagan temples (e.g., Dan. 1:8). Drinking alcohol is still a problem today for other reasons (not all "wine" was fermented). Some Christians have no problem with drinking alcohol in moderation because there is no NT commandment that expressly forbids it. Yet, Paul taught principles by which those with discernment understand that we should abstain from drinking alcohol.

That Paul told Timothy to "use a little wine" for his stomach's sake (1 Tim. 5:23) has nothing to do with this issue. That was medical advice, and the fact he told Timothy to do it proves that he was not in the habit of drinking wine.

We should abstain from alcohol because:
1) It has the power to enslave (1 Cor. 6:12) – it is dangerous (Prov. 20:1; 23:29-35).

2) It is does not glorify God (1 Cor. 10:31) – consider what it is associated with throughout the Bible (e.g., Gen. 9:21).
3) It is a bad testimony (1 Thess. 5:22).
4) It is not expedient to spiritual growth (1 Cor. 10:23).
5) It does not edify others (1 Cor. 10:23).
6) It may give someone who cannot handle it a green light to partake of it (Rom. 14:21).

(22) Hast thou faith? have it to thyself before God. Happy is he that condemneth not himself in that thing which he alloweth.

If we have the faith to practice what another brother condemns, we should keep it to ourselves before God and not flaunt our liberty before our weaker brother. There is happiness in doing things the right way and being thoughtful of others.

(23) And he that doubteth is damned if he eat, because he eateth not of faith: for whatsoever is not of faith is sin.

The word "damned" is used here in the sense of temporal condemnation (1 Cor. 11:26-34). To do something with a doubtful conscience is sin. Faith is knowing and believing what God said (Rom. 4:3-5; 10:17). If we don't know what God said on a matter, and our conscience tells us it's wrong, then we are to treat it as wrong until we have further light on the matter. "If it's doubtful, it's dirty" is a good principle to follow. You wouldn't eat or drink something that *might be* poisoned.

George Williams wrote, "Faith is dependence upon God. Every action which displaces that dependence in the conscience is an independent action and all such independence from God is sinful." (The Student's Commentary on the Holy Scriptures, pg. 874)

This is one of several verses in the Bible that plainly state what sin is.

1) An high look and proud heart (Prov. 21:4)
2) The thought of foolishness (Prov. 24:9)
3) Whatsoever is not of faith (Rom. 14:23)
4) Knowing to do good, but not doing it (Jam. 4:17)
5) The transgression of the law (1 Jn. 3:4)
6) All unrighteousness (I Jn. 5:17)

Romans 15

In the first part of this chapter Paul continues to deal with our conduct in relation to those who are weak in the faith (Rom. 14:1).

Am I Pleasing Myself or Others?

(1) We then that are strong ought to bear the infirmities of the weak, and not to please ourselves.
(2) Let every one of us please his neighbour for his good to edification.

Those who are strong in the faith are to minister to those who are weak; not look down on them (Gal. 6:1-3). If we are strong in the faith, we should be strong enough to bear the infirmities (i.e., weaknesses) of our weaker brethren. Those walking in love (Rom. 12:9; 13:8) seek to please others and not themselves (1 Cor. 10:33). We are to please others for their edification, but we are never to compromise the truth (Gal. 1:10).

(3) For even Christ pleased not himself; but, as it is written, The reproaches of them that reproached thee fell on me.
(4) For whatsoever things were written aforetime were written for our learning, that we through patience and comfort of the scriptures might have hope.

Study Notes

Our Master was the greatest servant. Christ did everything for the glory of God (Jn. 8:29) and the good of others (Matt. 20:28), no matter the reproach it brought Him. Christians are not to live for themselves (1 Tim. 4:10).

Paul quoted from the Psalms (69:9), and he did so many times in his epistles (3x's in this chapter). There is comfort and hope for the Body of Christ in the Psalms (Eph. 5:18-19). The OT is not about us, but it is for us (1 Cor. 9:9-10; 10:11; 2 Tim. 3:16). We get comfort and hope from the scriptures (Ps. 119:50), as we believe it (Rom. 15:13).

(5) Now the God of patience and consolation grant you to be likeminded one toward another according to Christ Jesus:
(6) That ye may with one mind and one mouth glorify God, even the Father of our Lord Jesus Christ.
(7) Wherefore receive ye one another, as Christ also received us to the glory of God.

Since God is patient with us, we should be patient with one another. We will be of one mind if we let the mind of Christ be in us (Phil. 2:1-5). Of course, this does not mean that we must have the same opinions about every little thing. The mind and the mouth are connected (2 Cor. 4:13). With one mind and mouth we should glorify God. It glorifies God for brethren to receive one another as Christ received us.

Christ's Ministry to Jews and Gentiles

The remainder of this chapter concerns three different ministries (v.8, 16, 27).

1) Christ's Ministry to Jews and Gentiles (vv.8-13)
2) Paul's Ministry to the Gentiles (vv.14-21)
3) The Gentile Churches' Ministry to the Jews (vv.22-33)

A Minister of the Circumcision

(8) Now I say that Jesus Christ was a minister of the circumcision for the truth of God, to confirm the promises made unto the fathers:
(9) And that the Gentiles might glorify God for his mercy; as it is written, For this cause I will confess to thee among the Gentiles, and sing unto thy name.
(10) And again he saith, Rejoice, ye Gentiles, with his people.
(11) And again, Praise the Lord, all ye Gentiles; and laud him, all ye people.
(12) And again, Esaias saith, There shall be a root of Jesse, and he that shall rise to reign over the Gentiles; in him shall the Gentiles trust.
(13) Now the God of hope fill you with all joy and peace in believing, that ye may abound in hope, through the power of the Holy Ghost.

What Paul says in this passage is based on what he said in the preceding passage concerning how those strong in the faith are to treat the weak. The issues that Paul has been addressing would be common in a church that has both Jews and Gentiles. He closed out the preceding passage exhorting the brethren to receive one another as Christ received us. His main point here is the fact Jesus Christ was a minister to the circumcision in no way meant that He did not also care for the Gentiles and purpose to bless them.

Study Notes

Paul quoted four prophecies (from each of the three main sections of the OT: law, prophets, and psalms) about the Kingdom Age and applied them spiritually to this present age. He used an OT principle to show that since God intends for both Jews and Gentiles to praise Him together, they ought to be doing that today in the Body of Christ.

Comparing Psalm 18:49 with Romans 15:9 defines Gentiles as "heathen" and Deuteronomy 32:43 with Romans 15:10 and Psalm 117:1 with Romans 15:11 defines Gentiles as "nations." The wording of OT quotes in the NT do not always match, but they are given by inspiration and there are typically things to learn by the differences.

The apostle Paul often applied OT scripture to this present age (v.4). He did it six times in this chapter. Hyperdispensationalists have a difficult time with Paul's use of the OT here. They claim that the mystery of the Body of Christ wasn't revealed until Acts 28, but Paul clearly taught it in epistles he wrote before Acts 28 (Rom. 12:4-5; 16:25; 1 Cor. 12:13; Gal. 3:27-28). Once the primary doctrinal interpretation of a passage is understood, we may also draw a secondary application so long as the application does not violate sound doctrine.

Notice in Paul's prayer (v.13) that joy, peace, and hope is dependent upon believing the word of God. He is the God of "patience and consolation" (v.5), "hope" (v.13), and "peace" (v.33).

God wants us to abound in the Christian life. The Holy Ghost makes our hope real to our hearts (Rom. 5:1-5). We don't have to wait until the kingdom is established to rejoice in Christ.

Earthly Ministry	Heavenly Ministry
Prophecy (Lk. 24:27, 44)	Mystery (Rom. 16:25)
Confirmation (Rom. 15:8)	Inauguration (Acts 26:16)
Primary Scriptures – The Four Gospels	Exclusive Scriptures – Paul's Epistles
Christ is the King of Israel (Jn. 1:49)	Christ is the Head of One Body (2 Cor. 5:16-17)
Dispensation of Law (Matt. 5:17-20; 23:1-3)	Dispensation of Grace (Rom. 6:14; Eph. 3:1-13)
Gospel of the Kingdom (Matt. 4:23)	Gospel of the Grace of God (Acts 20:24)
Difference Jew and Gentile (Matt. 15:21-28)	No Difference Jew and Gentile (Gal. 3:27-28)
Sent 12 to Israel (Matt. 10:5-6)	Sent Paul to the Gentiles (Rom. 11:13)
Signs Abound (Jn. 20:30-31)	Signs Ceased (1 Cor. 13:8-13)
Kingdom Commission (Mk. 16:15-18)	Grace Commission (2 Cor. 5:18-20)

Paul's Ministry to the Gentiles

(14) And I myself also am persuaded of you, my brethren, that ye also are full of goodness, filled with all knowledge, able also to admonish one another.

The flesh is not "full of goodness" (Rom. 3:12; 7:18), our goodness is found in Christ alone (Phile. 6). Based on the knowledge of the scripture, we can admonish one another. Learning the Bible should be about knowing God and serving others, not just obtaining knowledge (1 Cor. 8:1).

(15) Nevertheless, brethren, I have written the more boldly unto you in some sort, as putting you in mind, because of the grace that is given to me of God,
(16) That I should be the minister of Jesus Christ to the Gentiles, ministering the gospel of God, that the offering up of the Gentiles might be acceptable, being sanctified by the Holy Ghost.

(17) I have therefore whereof I may glory through Jesus Christ in those things which pertain to God.

(18) For I will not dare to speak of any of those things which Christ hath not wrought by me, to make the Gentiles obedient, by word and deed,

(19) Through mighty signs and wonders, by the power of the Spirit of God; so that from Jerusalem, and round about unto Illyricum, I have fully preached the gospel of Christ.

(20) Yea, so have I strived to preach the gospel, not where Christ was named, lest I should build upon another man's foundation:

(21) But as it is written, To whom he was not spoken of, they shall see: and they that have not heard shall understand.

This is one of many passages in which Paul, by inspiration of God, declares his authority as the apostle of the Gentiles (Rom. 11:13). God used his ministry to make many Gentiles obedient to the faith. We are obedient to the faith (Rom. 1:5) by faith (Rom. 16:26). He gave God all the glory for what He was doing through him (cf. v.20; Col. 1:28-29).

Paul went to the Jew first (Rom. 1:16) in the Acts period (see Rom. 11) but his primary ministry from the beginning was to the Gentiles (Acts 26:17). Christ chose Paul to be the pattern (1 Tim. 1:12-16) and spokesman (1 Cor. 11:1) for the Body of Christ in this present age and failure to understand this leads to much confusion and bad doctrine (2 Tim. 2:7).

Peter was NOT an apostle to the Gentiles (Matt. 19:28; Gal. 2:9). He did minister to some Gentiles (Acts 10), but his primary ministry was to the circumcision. There is no biblical evidence that Peter ever went to Rome as the Roman Catholic Church falsely claims. That Paul would not build upon another man's foundation (v.20) and that Peter is not mentioned in chapter 16 proves he was not in Rome. Peter preached Christ according to prophecy (1 Pet. 1:9-13), but Paul laid the foundation for this present age by preaching Christ according to the revelation of the mystery (Rom. 16:25; 1 Cor. 3:10).

The "gospel of God" was the foundational good news (Rom 1:1-4) that was common to both Peter (1 Pet. 4:17) and Paul's ministry. The gospel of Christ was the further revelation that Christ died for our sins. His death would not have accomplished salvation had He not be the Son of God and risen from the dead.

This passage proves that Paul did not do the signs of the kingdom because he said that he had been preaching the gospel of Christ (v.19), not the gospel of the kingdom. He had the signs of an apostle (2 Cor. 12:12). Notice in verse 18 that the preaching of the word comes first because it is more important than the signs.

That Paul "fully preached the gospel of Christ" means he preached the full message (Acts 20:20-21, 26-27; 1 Thess. 2:4) with his full being (Rom. 1:15) as he fulfilled his ministry (Acts 20:24; 2 Tim. 4:5-7). That Paul's ministry in Illyricum (Europe, NW of Philippi) is not recorded in the book of Acts proves that it is not an exhaustive and complete record of his ministry.

Once again (v.21), Paul spiritually applied a prophecy concerning the Kingdom Age (Isa. 52:15) to provide a principle for ministry. Paul had not visited Rome yet because there were already believers there. We should work to get the gospel to those who have never heard it (vv.20-21; 2 Cor. 10:12-18). If more preachers followed this principle, we would be doing a much better job evangelizing the world.

The Gentile Churches' Ministry to the Jews

(23) But now having no more place in these parts, and having a great desire these many years to come unto you;
(24) Whensoever I take my journey into Spain, I will come to you: for I trust to see you in my journey, and to be brought on my way thitherward by you, if first I be somewhat filled with your company.
(25) But now I go unto Jerusalem to minister unto the saints.

Paul wrote this epistle from Corinth (Rom. 16:23) when he was on his way to Jerusalem (Acts 20:2-3). After his visit to Jerusalem, he intended to visit Rome on his way to Spain. He had long desired to visit Rome (Rom. 1:8-15), but his ministry in other areas where Christ wasn't being preached had hindered him from getting there (comparing Rom. 1:13 with Rom. 15:22 defines "let" as "hindered"). The Bible does not say if he made it to Spain, but it is possible that he did between his two imprisonments in Rome. There is nothing wrong with making plans if we do so in submission to the Lord (1 Cor. 16:5-7).

(26) For it hath pleased them of Macedonia and Achaia to make a certain contribution for the poor saints which are at Jerusalem.
(27) It hath pleased them verily; and their debtors they are. For if the Gentiles have been made partakers of their

spiritual things, their duty is also to minister unto them in carnal things.
28 When therefore I have performed this, and have sealed to them this fruit, I will come by you into Spain.
29 And I am sure that, when I come unto you, I shall come in the fulness of the blessing of the gospel of Christ.

Paul took up a collection among the Gentile churches for the poor saints in Jerusalem (Acts 24:17; 1 Cor. 16:1-4; 2 Cor. 8-9; Gal. 2:10). This was not the first time he took an offering to Jerusalem (Acts 11:27-30). The churches started by Paul had believing Jews in them, but they were primarily made up of Gentiles (Rom. 16:4). The offering from the churches in Macedonia and Achaia were said to be from the Gentiles. This proves the churches of Corinth, Philippi, and Thessalonica were not primarily Jewish as some have suggested.

Why were there poor saints in Jerusalem? In the early Acts period, they had sold out and had all things common as they waited for the kingdom to be established (Acts 2:44-45; 4:34-35). The kingdom was postponed, a famine came, and the unbelieving Jews would not help them.

Why did Paul take up this offering?
 1) The promise he made (Gal. 2:8-10).
 2) His burden for the Jews (v.31; Rom. 9:1-3).
 3) The debt of the Gentiles.

In the immediate context Paul has been promoting fellowship between believing Jews and Gentiles. That the Gentiles are made partakers of Israel's "spiritual things" has to do with what Paul taught by the fig tree illustration (Rom. 11:16-24).

The poor saints in Jerusalem would be the branches that were not broken off and so the wild olive tree (Gentiles) was graffed in among them and became partakers of their spiritual blessings. For example, the Gentiles were hearing from Israel's scriptures how that Jesus was the prophesied Christ ("gospel of God"). Remember, the gospel by which we are saved is "according to the scriptures" (although it was not revealed in the OT, Gal. 1:11-12). In the Acts period those that believed on Christ were given spiritual sign gifts. All of this was to provoke the unbelieving Jews to jealousy and as a result some of them also believed. Because the Gentiles were partakers of Israel's spiritual blessings, the least they could do was minister to them in carnal things (i.e., give a contribution to meet material needs), which is a Bible principle (1 Cor. 9:11; Gal. 6:6).

Giving is a ministry and fruit of the Christian life (v.28; Phil. 4:17). Since God is the greatest giver (2 Cor. 8:9; 9:15), certainly his people should be cheerful givers! In the Bible, offerings are taken up for poor saints and the work of the ministry. It's too bad that many American churches waste millions of dollars on buildings.

(30) Now I beseech you, brethren, for the Lord Jesus Christ's sake, and for the love of the Spirit, that ye strive together with me in your prayers to God for me;
(31) That I may be delivered from them that do not believe in Judaea; and that my service which I have for Jerusalem may be accepted of the saints;
(32) That I may come unto you with joy by the will of God, and may with you be refreshed.
(33) Now the God of peace be with you all. Amen.

Study Notes

Paul was always praying or requesting prayer. We are to "strive together" (not against one another) for the faith of the gospel (Phil. 1:27) and in prayer for those who faithfully preach it (Eph. 6:18-20). Real prayer is a spiritual labor (Col. 4:12).

Note the Godhead in verse 30. There are many verses in Paul's epistles in which he mentions the Godhead together (e.g., 2 Cor. 13:14; Eph. 2:18).

The three prayer requests (vv.31-32) were answered, although probably not exactly as Paul expected.

1) "That I may be delivered from that do not believe in Judea" – He was arrested but not killed.
2) "that my service which I have for Jerusalem may be accepted of the saints" – It was.
3) "That I may come unto you with joy by the will of God" – He arrived in Rome by the will of God, but as a prisoner of the Lord. Some believe Paul was out of the will of God when he went to Jerusalem for the final time. We deal with that issue in our Acts commentary.

God is the God of "patience and consolation" (v.5), "hope" (v.13) and "peace" (v.33). The God of peace lives in all believers, but He will practically "be with" those who follow Paul's example (Phil. 4:9).

Paul concluded the main body of his letter at the end of this chapter. The last chapter contains three postscripts (Rom. 16:20, 24, 27).

Romans 16

In this final chapter Paul mentions thirty-five people by name (mostly Gentile names). He commends Phebe (vv.1-2), greets twenty-seven people (vv.3-16, only Aquila and Priscilla are mentioned by Paul in other passages), and he sends greetings from eight people that were with him at Corinth when he wrote the letter (vv.21-23).

Paul had probably not seen most of the saints he mentioned in a long time, and perhaps he had only heard about some of them, but they were on his mind because of how much he loved them and prayed for them. It is obvious that he genuinely appreciated all the saints and that he was not the "go it alone" type. God did not intend for believers to serve Him on our own. The Spirit gives us the desire for fellowship with other believers.

Paul was careful to greet others and he exhorted believers to greet one another in the local church. Every member should feel at home in the assembly. If we will not simply greet someone, we certainly will not pray for them.

A Commendation

(1) I commend unto you Phebe our sister, which is a servant of the church which is at Cenchrea:
(2) That ye receive her in the Lord, as becometh saints, and that ye assist her in whatsoever business she hath

need of you: for she hath been a succourer of many, and of myself also.

Phebe faithfully served the church at Cenchrea, which was a port of Corinth (Acts 18:18), and Paul wrote this epistle from Corinth. Perhaps Phebe was entrusted with the responsibility to carry this inspired letter all the way to Rome.

It is fitting for saints to receive one another considering how the Lord received us (Rom. 15:7).

By comparing Isaiah 49:8 with 2 Corinthians 6:2 we learn that "succoured" means "helped."

The corrupt modern versions call Phebe a "deaconess" but there is no such office in the Bible. The two offices in the local church are that of the bishop and deacon, and being the husband of one wife is one of the qualifications for both (1 Tim. 3:2, 12). The same Greek word (*diakonos*) is also translated "minister" (20x's) and "servant" (8x's). Every deacon is a servant and minister, but not all servants and ministers are deacons (Rom. 13:4; 2 Cor. 11:15).

There are no offices of leadership in the church for women. Some ignorantly accuse Paul of being against women because of his teaching on the role of women (e.g., 1 Tim. 2:9-15). Paul wrote the word of God, not his own opinions. The first person that Paul mentions in this chapter full of names is a woman (8 female names in this chapter). It is God's will for men to be leaders in the home, church, and society. Women are not inferior to men; they just have a different role. Of course, Christian women are to help in the Lord's work (v.6; Phil. 4:2-3).

Closing Greetings

(3) Greet Priscilla and Aquila my helpers in Christ Jesus:
(4) Who have for my life laid down their own necks: unto whom not only I give thanks, but also all the churches of the Gentiles.
(5) Likewise greet the church that is in their house. Salute my wellbeloved Epaenetus, who is the firstfruits of Achaia unto Christ.

Paul first met Aquila and Priscilla, who had lived in Rome, at Corinth (Acts 18:1-3). They worked together as tentmakers. This faithful married couple was a great blessing to Paul's ministry. They risked their lives to help him (probably in Ephesus during the riot), for which not only Paul but also the churches he started were very thankful. They went with Paul to Ephesus (1 Cor. 16:19) but later returned to Rome, and a church was meeting in their house. This explains why there were members of the Body of Christ in Rome before Paul went there. They evidently went back to Ephesus (2 Tim. 4:19). It is a great blessing to have couples like Aquilla and Priscilla in the church. Married couples and families should serve the Lord together (Phile. 1-2).

Paul had started many local churches by this point in his Acts ministry (Acts 20:3), and they were primarily made up of Gentile believers ("churches of the Gentiles"). This refutes the idea that Paul did not start ministering to the Gentiles until the end of the Acts period.

This chapter contains the first mention of the church in Paul's epistles (v.1, 4, 5, 14-16, 23). There is ONE Body (Rom. 12:4-5; 1 Cor. 12:13; Eph. 4:4), but many "churches." That God is building one spiritual church in this present age does not diminish the importance of the local church. The local church is to be a microcosm of the Body of Christ in a community (1 Tim. 3:14-16). Forty-seven of the sixty-one references to the church in Paul's epistles are about the local church. It is God's will that we be part of two churches: the Body of Christ for salvation (Rom. 6:3-4) and the local church for service. We can do far more together than we can on our own.

Some believe that churches today must meet in houses because the early church did not own their own buildings (Rom. 16:5; 1 Cor. 16:19; Col. 4:15; Phile. 1:2). The early churches did not have the opportunity to own their own building. A local church is an assembly of believers, where it meets is not the issue. It is not wrong for a church to buy property and have a building, but it is wrong for a church to emphasize the carnal over the spiritual. Paul certainly did not start "megachurches" that followed a business model of operations.

This is the only mention of Epaenetus, who was one of Paul's first converts in Achaia, which means he was part of the house of Stephanas (1 Cor. 16:15).

(6) Greet Mary, who bestowed much labour on us.
(7) Salute Andronicus and Junia, my kinsmen, and my fellowprisoners, who are of note among the apostles, who also were in Christ before me.

There are several women in the Bible with the name of Mary. All we know about this Mary is that she was in Rome and had labored to help Paul and his fellowlabourers.

That Andronicus and Junia were Paul's kinsman (v.11, 21) probably means that they were Jews (Rom. 9:3) and not his near relatives. At one point they had been in prison with Paul. That they were of "note among the apostles" could either mean they were apostles (in a secondary sense), or the apostles took notice of their ministry. They were in the little flock of believing Israel because they were "in Christ" before Paul was saved. During the transition period some of the kingdom saints heard and believed Paul's gospel and became members of the Body of Christ (e.g., Barnabas, Luke, and Silas).

Those who believe that the Body of Christ began historically before the salvation of Paul use verse 7 as a proof text. All who are in the Body of Christ are in Christ but not all who are in Christ are in the Body of Christ. Because of the cross of Christ, believing Israel was, and will be, in Christ redemptively (Isa. 45:24-25; Jn. 17:20-23; Eph. 1:10; Rev. 14:13). What makes the Body of Christ distinct from Israel is not that we are in Christ, but that Jews and Gentiles are in one spiritual Body with no distinction (Gal. 3:27-28). The basis of this one new man is the cross and shed blood of Christ (Eph. 2:16), but we get into the Body by the gospel revealed through Paul (Gal. 1:11-12; Eph. 3:6). The Bible does not explicitly state when the Body began historically but we know it was a mystery hid in God and first revealed through Paul (Eph. 3:1-12). The most important thing is to know what the Body of Christ is and how to get in it!

(8) Greet Amplias my beloved in the Lord.
(9) Salute Urbane, our helper in Christ, and Stachys my beloved.
(10) Salute Apelles approved in Christ. Salute them which are of Aristobulus' household.

As it is used in the Bible, "hope" is a certain expectation and anticipation of something God promised. Our blessed hope is to be caught up TOGETHER and glorified TOGETHER with Christ. In that day there will never be another division in the Body of Christ.

Verse 8 is a key verse concerning dispensational truth. Christ plainly said that He was sent to the lost sheep of the house of Israel, and He only ministered to a few Gentiles who were first a blessing to the Jews (Matt. 15:21-28). According to prophecy, the Gentiles are to be blessed through Israel's rise and glory (Isa. 60:1-3). The earthly ministry of Christ was about confirming what God promised the Jewish fathers, not revealing the mystery of this present age. Israel is God's earthly people and He promised them a land and world-wide kingdom over the nations. In the kingdom prophecies that Paul quotes (vv.9-12), the Gentiles praise God with Israel but there is still a distinction between them: they will not be in one Body in the earthly kingdom.

A comparison of verses 8 and 16 will help us immensely in understanding the Bible. There is a difference between the earthly ministry of Christ to Israel, and His heavenly ministry through Paul.

In this present age, as revealed through Paul's ministry, the Gentiles are blessed through the FALL of Israel (Rom. 11:12) and believing Jews and Gentiles are baptized by one Spirit into one spiritual Body wherein there are no earthly distinctions (Gal. 3:27-28).

(11) Salute Herodion my kinsman. Greet them that be of the household of Narcissus, which are in the Lord.
(12) Salute Tryphena and Tryphosa, who labour in the Lord. Salute the beloved Persis, which laboured much in the Lord.
(13) Salute Rufus chosen in the Lord, and his mother and mine.
(14) Salute Asyncritus, Phlegon, Hermas, Patrobas, Hermes, and the brethren which are with them.
(15) Salute Philologus, and Julia, Nereus, and his sister, and Olympas, and all the saints which are with them.

Paul mentioned twenty names in these nine verses, and only Rufus is mentioned in another passage (Mk. 15:21), but it is probably not the same man. What did Paul mean by "his mother and mine?" Perhaps his mother treated Paul like one of her own. It is doubtful that he was Paul's brother.

Our labor must be "in the Lord" (6x's, "in Christ" 4x's) for it to be of any real and eternal value (v.12; 1 Cor. 15:58). Notice that the people Paul greeted did not have important titles (Job 32:21-22; Lk. 11:43), but they were simply servants, helpers, and labourers (1 Cor. 3:5-9).

(16) Salute one another with an holy kiss. The churches of Christ salute you.

Greeting one another with a "holy kiss" (v.16; 1 Cor. 16:20; 2 Cor. 13:12; 1 Thess. 5:26) was the custom of that time and culture. In America today believers practice the holy handshake.

The "Church of Christ" claims they are the true church and boast that their name is in the Bible (v.16). Their slogan is, "We speak where the Bible speaks, and we are silent where the Bible is silent." Yet nowhere does the Bible say, "the Church of Christ." It does say, "the church of God" seven times, but that name has been claimed by a Pentecostal denomination. Paul also referred to the "churches of the Gentiles" (v.4), "churches of God" (1 Cor. 11:16), "churches of the saints" (1 Cor. 14:33), "churches of Galatia" (1 Cor. 16:1), "churches of Asia" (1 Cor. 16:19), and the "churches of Macedonia" (2 Cor. 8:1). God never said that a church must be called by a certain name. It is immature to get caught up in names, because the main issue is our doctrine. The "Church of Christ" preaches a false gospel by requiring water baptism for salvation (1 Cor. 1:17). Ironically, Paul brings up false teachers in the very next verse.

A Closing Warning

After exhorting the saints at Rome to salute one another (v.16) Paul warns them about those they need to avoid. The Bible is a balanced book that gives both positive exhortations and negative warnings. Contrary to what many think today, we are not to receive just anybody and everybody in the assembly. Christian unity and fellowship are important, but we will not be able to protect it and maintain it if we fail to heed this warning. Those who obey it will be accused of being divisive, but not all division is bad (Jn. 7:43; 9:16; 10:19).

(17) Now I beseech you, brethren, mark them which cause divisions and offences contrary to the doctrine which ye have learned; and avoid them.

(18) For they that are such serve not our Lord Jesus Christ, but their own belly; and by good words and fair speeches deceive the hearts of the simple.

This passage contains the first mention of Satan in Paul's epistles, and it reveals his primary strategy against the Body of Christ in this present age. Paul never warns us about devil possession in his epistles, but he warned us many times about the danger of false doctrine. The battlefield in spiritual warfare is the mind (2 Cor. 11:3). Satan has ministers that preach another Jesus, spirit, and gospel (2 Cor. 11:4, 13-15). He also uses corrupt versions of the Bible (2 Cor. 2:17).

Paul pleaded with the brethren to heed his warning. Notice that Paul did not say, "IF some cause divisions and offences" because he takes it for granted that it will happen (Acts 20:28-31). The devil will always try to get the leaven of false doctrine (Gal. 5:9) into a Bible-believing and gospel-preaching church that rightly divides the word of truth.

Paul did not say "mark and avoid all those who disagree with your opinions and preferences." As we saw in chapters 14 and 15, we are to receive one another concerning disagreements about doubtful things. The standard by which we know who to mark and follow and who we are to mark and avoid is the sound doctrine of what Christ revealed through Paul for the Body of Christ in this present age (Phil. 3:17-21).

Paul emphasized the absolute necessity and importance of "sound doctrine" (16x's in the Pastoral Epistles) and yet many preachers today minimize it. Sound doctrine is life-changing when it is believed and obeyed from the heart (Rom. 6:17; 2 Tim.

1:13; 3:10). It will save us from the deception and apostasy of the last days (1 Tim. 4:16; 2 Tim. 3:13-17).

The doctrine Paul is referring to in particular is justification and sanctification by faith without the works of the law, which is the major theme of this epistle (1 Tim. 1:3-11). We are not to tolerate those that preach another gospel (Gal. 1:6-12).

Heresy is promoting false doctrine to the point of causing divisions (1 Cor. 11:18-19; Gal. 5:20). After two admonitions we are to reject the heretic (Titus 3:10-11).

- **"mark them"** – Publicly identify them to warn others (e.g., 1 Tim. 1:18-20; 2 Tim. 1:15; 4:14-15).
- **"avoid them"** – Shun them. We are to separate from false teachers (2 Tim. 2:15-21). Bible-believers do not persecute heretics, but false religion has always persecuted Bible-believers.

Paul explained why we are to mark and avoid them (v.18). They are not the servants of Christ (although they pretend to be), and they will deceive the hearts of the simple (those who are unlearned in sound doctrine) if we allow them in our assembly. This verse gives us two identifying marks of false teachers.

1) Motive – Selfish gain (Titus 1:10-11).
2) Method – Smooth talk; flattery (Ps. 55:21; Prov. 5:3; Isa. 30:10; Col. 2:4). Satan beguiled the woman with a positive approach (2 Cor. 11:3). Simple (the opposite of wise) people care more about tone than truth (Prov. 14:15; 22:3; 27:6, 12). Paul used great plainness of speech (1 Cor. 2:1-5; 2 Cor. 3:12; 10:10; 11:6).

(19) For your obedience is come abroad unto all men. I am glad therefore on your behalf: but yet I would have you wise unto that which is good, and simple concerning evil.

(20) And the God of peace shall bruise Satan under your feet shortly. The grace of our Lord Jesus Christ be with you. Amen.

Paul had confidence that they would obey his instruction because they had already proven to be faithful (Rom. 1:8), but he was still compelled to give them this important warning. We are not to dialogue with false teachers and seek to understand their doctrine. False doctrine is EVIL (1 Cor. 15:33; Phil. 3:2; 2 Tim. 3:13).

Those who are not grounded in the foundational doctrine that Paul taught in this epistle lack spiritual wisdom and therefore vulnerable to deception. The best way to identify false doctrine is to be rooted and grounded in sound doctrine. We must focus on that which is good (Rom. 12:9; 1 Cor. 14:20). It is the holy scriptures that make us wise unto that which is good (Ps. 119:30; 2 Tim. 3:13-17).

Christ defeated Satan through His death, burial, and resurrection (Gen. 3:15; Col. 2:15; Heb. 2:14) but his final execution is yet future (Rev. 20:1-3, 10). Therefore, he is still actively opposing the Lord and His people.

The Body of Christ has victory over Satan:
1) Positional Victory (Acts 26:18; Col. 1:13)
2) Practical Victory – God will give us victory over Satan in our walk and warfare when we put on the spiritual

armour that He has given us (Eph. 6:10-20). The God of peace will bruise Satan, who seeks to disrupt the peace within a church, under the feet of those who believe and obey Paul's doctrine and instruction.

3) Permanent Victory – We will have permanent victory over Satan at the coming of the Lord. Being glorified we will never "give place to the devil" (Eph. 4:27) again. The Body of Christ is God's agent to reconcile the government of the heavenly places (Col. 1:16, 20). We will fill the vacant seats of authority after Satan and his angels are cast out of the second heaven. Therefore, Satan hates the "revelation of the mystery" (v.25) and works hard to keep the saints blinded to this glorious truth (1 Cor. 2:8).

Paul refers to God as the "God of peace" four times (Rom. 15:33; Phil. 4:9; 1 Thess. 5:23) and the "Lord of peace" (2 Thess. 3:16). Peace is the fruit of righteousness (Isa. 32:17). There will be no peace on earth until the second coming of Christ. Until then, we can personally enjoy:

- Peace with God (Rom. 5:1)
- Peace of God (Phil. 4:7; Col. 3:15)
- Peaceable life (Rom. 12:18)

Closing Salutations

(21) Timotheus my workfellow, and Lucius, and Jason, and Sosipater, my kinsmen, salute you.

(22) I Tertius, who wrote this epistle, salute you in the Lord.

(23) Gaius mine host, and of the whole church, saluteth you. Erastus the chamberlain of the city saluteth you, and Quartus a brother.

Paul mentioned Timothy many times in his epistles, and he had only good things to say about his son in the faith. He was his faithful "workfellow" (1 Cor. 16:10). Real ministry is WORK!

In this chapter Paul referred to six brethren as his kinsmen (Jews, Rom. 9:3): three at Rome (v.7, 11) and three with him at Corinth. Lucius was from Antioch (Acts 13:1), Jason was from Thessalonica (Acts 17:1-9), and Sosipater was from Berea (likely the same man called Sopater, Acts 20:4).

Tertius (only mention) wrote the words of Romans as Paul spoke them by the Holy Ghost (Jer. 36:4; 2 Pet. 1:21). Paul typically did not write his letters with his own hand, but he signed his name on all his epistles as a token of their authenticity (1 Cor. 16:21; 2 Thess. 2:2; 3:17).

Both Gaius (1 Cor. 1:14) and Erastus (2 Tim. 4:20) are mentioned in connection with Corinth. Paul wrote this epistle from Corinth during his three-month stay there on his way to Jerusalem (Acts 20:2-3). Erastus was the city manager, and Quartus was probably a slave since his name was a number, yet they were members of the same Body (Gal. 3:27-28).

Paul opened and closed his epistles with "grace." Christ gave him the gospel of the grace of God, and he is the spokesman for this present age of grace. That is why he said more about the grace of God than all the other Bible writers combined!

Closing Doxology

(25) Now to him that is of power to stablish you according to my gospel, and the preaching of Jesus Christ,

according to the revelation of the mystery, which was kept secret since the world began,
(26) But now is made manifest, and by the scriptures of the prophets, according to the commandment of the everlasting God, made known to all nations for the obedience of faith:
(27) To God only wise, be glory through Jesus Christ for ever. Amen. Written to the Romans from Corinthus, and sent by Phebe servant of the church at Cenchrea.

There is no biblical evidence that Paul added this third postscript (Rom. 15:33; 16:20, 24) after he arrived in Rome as the Acts 28 Dispensationalists claim. They came up with that ridiculous idea to support their false view that Paul did not receive the revelation of the mystery until after Acts 28. Paul wrote about the Body of Christ in the epistles he wrote during the Acts period (e.g., 1 Cor. 4:1; 10:17; 12:13; 2 Cor. 12:7; Gal. 3:27-28).

It is "God only wise" (v.27) who has the power to "stablish" us through Jesus Christ, and He commanded that it be accomplished through three things.

There is a distinction in the KJB between the similar words "establish" (Rom. 1:11, to set up) and "stablish" (Rom. 16:25, to make stable what has been set up, Col. 2:6-7). The Oxford English Dictionary says that "stablish" became a variant of "establish" but notes that "From the 16th century there seems to have been a tendency to confine the use of the form stablish to those uses in which the relation of meaning to *stable* (adj.) is apparent, i.e., where the notion is rather 'to strengthen or support (something existing)' than 'to found or set up.'

Study Notes

1) **"my gospel"** – Paul called it "my gospel" (3x's, Rom. 2:16; 2 Tim. 2:8) because Christ personally and directly revealed it to him (Gal. 1:11-12), and committed it to his trust (1 Cor. 9:17; 1 Tim. 1:11). He could not have been saved under the gospel of the kingdom since he blasphemed the Holy Ghost (Matt. 12:31-32; 1 Tim. 1:12-16). The gospel of God was promised afore in the OT (Rom. 1:1-4), but Paul received a further revelation concerning what Christ accomplished through His death, burial, and resurrection. The gospel of our salvation is explained in detail in Romans 3 through 5, and it is summed up in 1 Corinthians 15:3-4. Paul is the first one to glory in the cross (Gal. 6:14) and preach it as good news. We are saved the moment we when we believe the gospel of the grace of God (Eph. 1:13) but believers need to be grounded in the truth of the gospel that we might enjoy "much assurance" (1 Thess. 1:5).

There is also a broader sense in which Paul's gospel could refer to all the doctrine that Christ revealed through him.

2) **"the preaching of Jesus Christ according to the revelation of the mystery"** – A "mystery" in the Bible is not something we cannot understand, but rather it is a secret that cannot be known until it is made manifest. God used the apostle Paul as a "wise masterbuilder" to lay the foundation for this present age (1 Cor. 3:10-11). The twelve apostles preached Jesus Christ according to prophecy (Lk. 1:67-75; Acts 3:19-21). The mystery that Christ revealed through Paul concerning this present age is the Body of Christ (Eph. 3:1-12; Col. 1:24-27). There are also other mysteries associated with it such as the rapture

(1 Cor. 4:1; 15:51-52). The "but now" passages in Paul's epistles prove dispensational truth (Rom. 3:21; Eph. 2:13; Col. 1:26).

3) **"the scriptures of the prophets"** – Some dispensational teachers wrongly change verse 27 to say, "prophetic writings" and claim Paul was referring to his own writings. Based on the many times Paul referred to the OT in this epistle, we know he is talking about the OT prophets. We need the whole Bible to be stablished (2 Tim. 3:16-17) because there are doctrines and moral principles in the OT that still apply in this age, and we learn how to rightly divide by comparing prophecy with the mystery.

Paul followed the order of these three things in this epistle:
1) Paul's gospel (Rom. 3-5)
2) Revelation of the mystery (Rom. 6-8; 12:4-5)
3) Scriptures of the prophets (Rom. 9-11; 15:1-13)

Paul's Church Epistles are laid out in the same order.
1) Paul's Gospel – Romans through Galatians
2) Revelation of the Mystery – Ephesians through Colossians
3) Scriptures of the prophets – Thessalonians (contrasts rapture with second coming)

That we understand the commission Christ gave the twelve apostles (Matt. 28:19-20; Mk. 16:15-18) concerns the gospel of the kingdom and is therefore not our commission does not mean we do not believe in "world missions." The everlasting God has commanded that His truth be made known to "all nations" (Rom.

1:5). God used Paul's ministry to get the gospel to "all the world" (Col. 1:6) and "every creature" (Col. 1:23) in the first century.

The mystery of the Body of Christ is a great demonstration of the wisdom of God (Eph. 3:10). Paul called God the "only wise" (1 Tim. 1:17) because all true wisdom comes from Him (Rom. 11:33-36).

By comparing verse 27 with Romans 1:5 we learn that "obedience to the faith" is the "obedience OF faith." The only way to obey the gospel of the grace of God is to believe it. Those who try to do works for salvation are not obeying the gospel (Rom. 4:5). Salvation by God's grace through faith in the finished work of Christ means that God gets all the glory (Eph. 2:8-9).

The Most Important Question

ARE YOU SAVED?

This question should receive a "Yes" or "No" answer, but it almost never does. Some of the most common responses are:
- I'm doing the best I can.
- I prayed the sinner's prayer.
- I've made Jesus the Lord of my life.
- I believe in God.
- I've been baptized.
- I'm a church member.
- I keep the commandments.
- I am basically a good person.
- I walked the aisle and prayed through.
- I've always been a Christian.
- I've never done anything really bad.

None of these responses properly answer the question. People give these kinds of responses because they evidently do not understand the question. The question, "Are you saved?" asks whether or not you have trusted Christ's shed blood on the cross as the payment for your sins. It is not asking about any works that you can do. The responses listed above refer to what a person does, but salvation is only offered on the basis of what Christ has already done for us.

The gospel of our salvation (Eph. 1:13) is clearly stated by the apostle Paul.

3 For I delivered unto you first of all that which I also received, how that Christ died for our sins according to the scriptures;

4 And that he was buried, and that he rose again the third day according to the scriptures. (1 Cor. 15:3-4)

The blood of Christ has purchased what we could not earn ourselves.

In whom we have redemption through his blood, even the forgiveness of sins: (Col. 1:14)

We cannot be good enough to earn salvation because "there is none righteous" (Rom. 3:10) and "all have sinned" (Rom. 3:23). The "wages of sin is death" (Rom. 6:23). Those who die lost will spend eternity in "the lake of fire" (Rev. 20:15).

In order to be saved, we must stop trusting ourselves and trust the blood payment that Christ has already made on our behalf!

8 For by grace are ye saved through faith; and that not of yourselves: it is the gift of God:
9 Not of works, lest any man should boast. (Eph. 2:8-9)

Jesus Christ fully accomplished our salvation through His death, burial, and resurrection. Therefore, the free gift of salvation can only be received by faith alone in His finished work.

Therefore being justified by faith, we have peace with God through our Lord Jesus Christ: (Rom. 5:1)

If you will trust Jesus Christ as your Saviour, you can enjoy "much assurance" (1 Thess. 1:5) that you are saved and on your way to heaven.

More From the Author

Study Notes on Basic Bible Truth
Study Notes on the King James Bible
Study Notes on Dispensational Truth
Study Notes on Books of the Bible
Study Notes on Acts
Study Notes on Colossians
Study Notes on The Epistles of Peter

Links to purchase the Study Notes books are found on our church website (click on Books and Tracts under Resources).

For hundreds of Bible studies and messages in audio, video, and written format, please visit:

www.hopebiblechurchga.com

Hope Bible Church
199 Four Points Rd.
Jackson, GA 30233

Printed by Amazon Italia Logistica S.r.l.
Torrazza Piemonte (TO), Italy